The Best of Philly Sports

Amazing Moments and Stories in Philadelphia Sports History

Joe DeCamara

TRIUMPH BOOKS

Library of Congress Cataloging-in-Publication Data available upon request.

This book is available in quantity at special discounts for your group or organization. For further information, contact:

Triumph Books LLC
814 North Franklin Street
Chicago, Illinois 60610
(312) 337-0747
www.triumphbooks.com

Printed in U.S.A.

ISBN: 978-1-63727-948-9
Design by Patricia Frey

Front cover photos: Focus on Sport/Getty Images (Bobby Clarke), Neil Leifer/NBAE/Getty Images (Julius Irving), Charles Krupa/AP Photo (Brad Lidge and Carlos Ruiz), Chris Szagola/AP Photo (Saquan Barkley)

Author photo: Michael DiSanto

Cover design: Jon Hahn

This book is dedicated to all young Philadelphia sports fans.

I want to entertain you with the greatest moments and stories from our past. There have been so many legendary players and incredible teams through the years in Philadelphia sports. Some of these stories happened in your lifetime, but most of them occurred before you were born. Your parents, grandparents, great-grandparents, and perhaps even your great-great grandparents were thrilled when these events happened in their lifetime. Now you can enjoy them too!

—Joe DeCamara

CONTENTS

PHILLIES

- Whiz Kids Win the 1950 Pennant on the Last Day of the Regular Season 8
- Jim Bunning Throws a Perfect Game 10
- Rick Wise Does Something No One Else Has Ever Done 11
- Steve Carlton's Season for the Ages 13
- Phillies Rule the NL East Three Straight Years in the 1970s 15
- 1980: The Phillies Finally Win the World Series 16
- Wheeze Kids Make One More Push in 1983 21
- Mike Schmidt Hits His 500th Home Run 22
- '93 Phils Go from Worst to First 24
- Back-to-Back MVPs, "the Team to Beat," and Overcoming Seven Down with 17 to Go 27
- The Championship Drought Is Over; Phillies Win the 2008 World Series 30
- Roy Halladay's Amazing Season 33
- 2022 Phillies Bring Red October Back to Citizens Bank Park 35

FLYERS

- The Founding of the Organization 40
- Flyers Win the Stanley Cup in 1974 and 1975 41
- America Is Proud as the Flyers Defeat the Soviet Red Army Team 45
- Reggie Leach Sets a Franchise Record for Goals in a Season 46
- Flyers Go 35 Straight Games Unbeaten 47
- Incredible Runs in 1985 and 1987 48
- A Goalie Scores 50
- The Legion of Doom Thrills Fans; Eric Lindros Tears Through the East in 1997 51
- Keith Primeau Scores in the Fifth Overtime 53
- Down 3–0 / 3–0 Flyers Complete an Amazing Comeback ... and Reach the Finals 54

SIXERS

- Trading For Wilt Chamberlain 58
- Sixers Dominate on Their Way to the 1967 Championship. 59
- Julius Erving Comes to Philly; Team Goes Straight to the Finals. 61
- Sixers Get to the 1980 Finals
  During an Unbelievable Year in Philly Sports 63
- A Game 7 Win in Boston 64
- ’83 Sixers Romp Through the NBA for the Title 66
- A Special Retirement Season for Dr. J 69
- The Great Charles Barkley 70
- Winning the 1996 Draft Lottery;
  Selecting Allen Iverson No. 1 Overall. 72
- 2001 Sixers Prove AI, Larry Brown, and Heart Can Take You Far 74
- The Immensely Talented Joel Embiid. 78

EAGLES

- Steve Van Buren Leads the 1948 and
  1949 Eagles to the Championship. 82
- Chuck Bednarik Plays Both Ways
  as the Eagles Win the Title in 1960 84
- The Meadowlands: A Place Where Miracles Happen. 85
- Dick Vermeil’s 1980 Eagles Beat Dallas
  in the NFC Championship Game 89
- The Incredible Reggie White 91
- 1991 Eagles Defense Ranks No. 1 Across the Board. 93
- Two Thrilling Playoff Victories in the 1990s 94
- Fourth-and-26 96
- 2004 Eagles Dominate the NFC. 98
- Making the Playoffs in Dramatic Fashion in 2008 101
- The Eagles Finally Win the Super Bowl 103
- Birds Soar in 2022 108
- Saquon Barkley’s Extraordinary Season
  Helps the Eagles Leap to the Top Again 109

THE BIG FIVE

- Tom Gola Shines as La Salle Wins the 1954 NCAA Championship..... 118
- Penn Makes the 1979 NCAA Final Four 119
- Freshman Mark Macon and Coach John Chaney Lead Temple to No. 1 in the Land..... 120
- Jameer Nelson, Phil Martelli, and St. Joe's Perfect Regular Season 123
- Villanova Plays a Game for the Ages Under Rollie Massimino ... and Wins Two More Titles Years Later with Jay Wright..... 125

ADDITIONAL MOMENTS AND STORIES

- The Penn Relays..... 130
- The Army-Navy Game 131
- Connie Mack's Philadelphia A's Win Five World Series..... 133
- John B. Kelly, Sr. Brings Glory to Philadelphia in the Olympics..... 134
- Philadelphia Warriors Win Two NBA Championships 135
- Wilt Scores 100 Points in a Game 137
- The Legendary Smokin' Joe Frazier..... 139
- Cathy Rush Leads Immaculata to a Three-Peat..... 141
- The Remarkable Carl Lewis 142
- Smarty Jones' Magical Run in the Kentucky Derby and Preakness..... 144
- The Amazing Bernard Hopkins..... 146
- Mo'ne Davis Stars in the Little League World Series..... 147
- Carli Lloyd Dominates on the World Stage 149
- The Champion Spirit of Dawn Staley 150

ADDENDUM

- Philadelphia Sports Hall of Famers..... 153

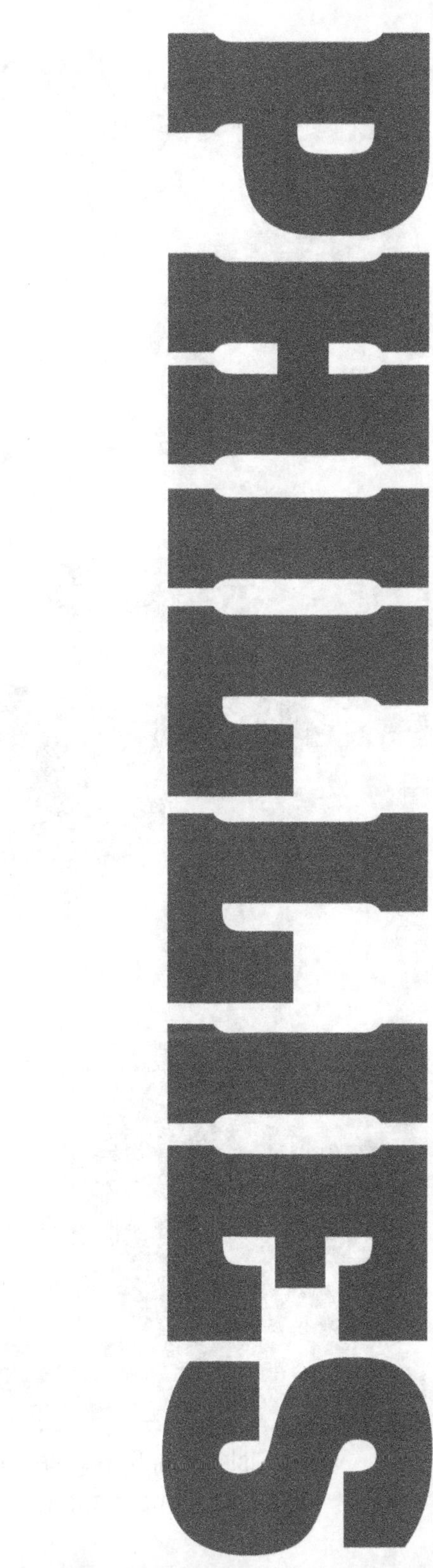
PHILLIES

Dick Sisler (No. 8) is greeted by his teammates after hitting one of the most important home runs in Phillies history. (AP Images)

Whiz Kids Win the 1950 Pennant on the Last Day of the Regular Season

1950 WAS SPECIAL FOR PHILLIES FANS. In order to understand why, it is key to know Phillies history prior to 1950. The Phils began play in 1883. The World Series did not exist until 1903. The Phils did not reach the World Series until 1915 when star pitcher Grover Cleveland Alexander led them there with a 31–10 record and a 1.22 ERA! But they lost to Boston. In the 1920s, 1930s, and 1940s the Phillies were terrible. Despite having the great Chuck Klein for half those years (he won an MVP Award and a Triple Crown), the Phils had a winning record only twice in 30 years. Until '50 the Phils had reached the World Series only once. Fans were starving for a winner.

The 1950 Phillies were a shock to baseball. Many of the players were young, and fans started calling them the "Whiz Kids." With future Hall of Famers Richie Ashburn and Robin Roberts, plus slugger Del Ennis and pitcher Jim Konstanty, who won the NL MVP Award, the Phils played excellent under manager Eddie Sawyer. Entering the final day of the regular season they led the Brooklyn Dodgers by one game. The clubs were set to face each other at Brooklyn's legendary Ebbets Field. A Dodgers win would force a three-game playoff; a Phillies win would send the Phils to the World Series. The Dodgers were loaded with stars such as Jackie Robinson, Pee Wee Reese, Roy Campanella, Gil Hodges, and Duke Snider. For the critical game Brooklyn started All-Star pitcher Don Newcombe. The Phils went with Roberts.

In the bottom of the ninth inning with the game tied 1–1, the Phils were in trouble as Brooklyn had runners on first and second with nobody out. Slugger Duke Snider hit a single up the middle, but in one of the biggest defensive plays in Phillies history centerfielder Richie Ashburn threw Dodgers baserunner Cal Abrams out at home plate! Roberts then recorded the next two outs sending the game to extra innings! In the top of the 10th, with two runners on, in one of the most exciting Phillies moments ever, Dick Sisler hit a three-run home run giving the Phils a 4–1 lead! In the bottom of the 10th, Roberts, pitching the entire way, retired the Dodgers to end the game! The Whiz Kids had won the National League pennant! Fans back in Philadelphia celebrated as the Phillies advanced to the World Series for just the second time in franchise history!

Unfortunately, the Phils lost the 1950 World Series to the New York Yankees. Despite that, the Whiz Kids remain one of Philadelphia's most legendary teams.

Jim Bunning Throws a Perfect Game

1964 IS A VERY TOUGH YEAR FOR PHILLIES FANS to think about because they were devastated when the Phils blew a 6½ game lead with 12 games left to lose out on the chance to go to the World Series. It remains to this day perhaps the single most disappointing turn of events in Philadelphia sports history. But 1964 was not all bad as the Phillies were in first place in the National League for the majority of the season, with stars Dick Allen (a future Hall of Famer who won the '64 Rookie of the Year Award), Johnny Callison, Jim Bunning (another future Hall of Famer), and Chris Short leading the way. There were many great moments, including Callison's thrilling ninth-inning homer to win the All-Star Game for the NL! But no moment was better than Bunning's perfect game, only the seventh in MLB history, and the first in the NL since 1880! A perfect game is so rare because the pitcher pitches the entire game without allowing the other team to get a hit, a walk, or to reach base in any way.

On Father's Day, Bunning, a father of seven kids at the time, pitched the game of his life, dominating the Mets at Shea Stadium in New York. He retired the first 26 Mets batters he faced, striking out nine of them. In the bottom of the ninth inning with the Phils leading 6–0, Bunning needed to get the next batter out to record the perfect game. Mets fans would not normally root for a Phillies player, but many New York fans stood and cheered for Bunning to make history in front of them.

Mets batter John Stephenson hoped to break up Bunning's bid for perfection. Bunning went into his windup and threw the first pitch … strike one. He went into his windup and threw the second pitch … strike two. Now Mets fans were cheering for the Phils pitcher even louder. But his next two pitches were both balls. The count was 2-2. Bunning took a little extra time out on the mound collecting his thoughts while getting ready to throw the next pitch. He went into his wind-up, threw the pitch, and … Stephenson swung and missed! Bunning had done it! He had thrown a perfect game! Bunning pounded his glove in excitement as teammates rushed toward him to congratulate him!

Bunning was elected to the Baseball Hall of Fame in 1996! After his playing days were over, he went on to a distinguished career in government, serving 12 years in the US House of Representatives and another 12 years as a US Senator! Bunning's No. 14 is one of the few uniform numbers ever retired by the Phillies!

Rick Wise Does Something No One Else Has Ever Done

IN THE LATE 1960s AND EARLY 1970s the Phillies struggled a lot as a team. They had losing records for seven straight seasons and gave fans little hope for glory. But in June of 1971 something glorious happened, as pitcher Rick Wise turned in a performance so unbelievable it may be the best game any player has ever played in Major League Baseball history! The reason is simple: not only did Wise accomplish the great feat of throwing a no-hitter versus the Cincinnati Reds, but he also hit two home runs in the same game!

The amazing accomplishment happened in Wise's seventh season in Philly. Entering 1971, Wise had a career record of 58 wins and 62 losses. He had been an average pitcher up until that point. But on this June night in '71, Wise was beyond spectacular. Facing a loaded Reds lineup that included star players such as Pete Rose, Johnny Bench, Tony Pérez, and George Foster, Wise pitched a masterful game. He retired the Reds in the first four innings without allowing a hit. Then, in the top of the fifth, Wise hit a home run off of Reds pitcher Ross Grimsley. Wise retired the Reds without giving up a hit in the bottom of the fifth, sixth, and seventh. Momentum was building for a possible no-hitter. In the top of the eighth inning, Wise connected again for his second homer of the night!

In the bottom of the eighth, Wise did not allow the Reds a hit. He entered the bottom of the ninth with a 4–0 lead and a chance to pitch a no-hitter. Wise retired the first two hitters in the ninth, but the next batter was the great Pete Rose, who was one of the best players in baseball. Years later Rose would star for the Phils, and later he would become the all-time hits leader in baseball history. But on this night in 1971, Rose stood as a tough out for Wise to secure a no-hitter. Wise and Rose battled with the count going to three balls and two strikes. Wise then went into his wind-up and threw a fastball, and Rose connected, hitting a sharp line drive, but it went right to third baseman John Vukovich, who caught the ball! Wise had pitched a no-hitter! His teammates rushed to celebrate with him! To this day Wise remains the only player in MLB history to throw a no-hitter and hit two home runs in the same game! Yes, perhaps the greatest game ever played by anyone in baseball history!

Steve Carlton's Season for the Ages

PRIOR TO THE 1972 SEASON THE PHILLIES MADE A BOLD MOVE trading Rick Wise to St. Louis for pitcher Steve Carlton. In time it proved to be one of the best trades in the history of Philadelphia sports. In his first season with the Phils, "Lefty," as he was called, put together one of the most spectacular individual seasons ever. Part of what made his season so extraordinary was how exceptional he pitched. The other main factor was how bad the Phillies were, finishing with the third-worst record in baseball. Carlton constantly had to overcome a truly terrible team around him to win his starts.

In his first start of the season Carlton pitched eight innings and gave up only two runs as the Phils won the game. He then won his next two starts with complete-game shutouts, raising his record to 3–0. In May, Carlton kept his ERA under 3.00, but with little run support from the Phillies offense Carlton lost five times that month. On June 1, his record was 5–6.

But in June Carlton's season really took off. He won on June 7 versus Houston, and then won an astounding 14 straight decisions in a row after that! Carlton's record on August 17 was 20–6. He continued to pitch great the rest of the season, winning some and losing some, but the Phillies bad offense made it hard for him to win as many games as he deserved to win given how well he was pitching. In one game Carlton gave up only two runs while pitching all 11 innings in a Phils loss.

When the season was over the final tally of Lefty's year was remarkable: a 27–10 record, a 1.97 ERA, 346⅓ innings pitched, 30 complete games, eight shutouts, and 310 strikeouts! Carlton's 27 wins for a team that won only 59 games set a Major League Baseball record as he was the winning pitcher in 45.7 percent of the Phils wins! For his efforts Carlton won the National League Cy Young Award as the league's top pitcher! It was the first of four times he would win the award!

Steve Carlton won four Cy Young Awards with the Phillies. His 329 wins are the second most by a left-handed pitcher in baseball history. (David Durochik/ AP Images)

Carlton became one of the greatest pitchers of all time. He helped the Phils reach the playoffs six times and was the best pitcher on the club's 1980 World Series winning team. He notched his 300th win in 1983, and finished his career with 329 wins, the second most by a left-handed pitcher in baseball history! Carlton was inducted into the Baseball Hall of Fame in 1994!

Phillies Rule the NL East Three Straight Years in the 1970s

FOLLOWING THE PHILS TRIP TO THE 1950 WORLD SERIES, fans endured many disappointing seasons over the next quarter-century. The club finished over .500 only twice from 1951 to 1961. They completely blew the pennant in 1964. And they were again below .500 each year from 1968 to 1974. With the possible exception of 1915–17, by the mid-1970s in the roughly 90 years the Phils had existed, they never put together what could be described as a good era of Phillies baseball.

But in 1966 the Phils made a key move that would benefit them for years when they elevated scout Paul Owens to run the club's farm system (the minor leagues). In 1972 Owens was hired as the team's general manager. During his time overseeing the farm system and as GM, Owens worked closely with Dallas Green, who helped with player evaluations and development. Together Owens, who was nicknamed "The Pope," and Green improved various aspects of the Phillies organization.

By the mid-1970s the fruits of their labor began to show. The Phils' lineup featured Mike Schmidt, Greg Luzinski, Larry Bowa, Bob Boone, Garry Maddox, Dave Cash, and Jay Johnstone. They even brought back slugger Dick Allen, who starred with the club in the 1960s. The pitching was led by the remarkable Steve Carlton, but also featured Jim Lonborg, Larry Christenson, Ron Reed, Gene Garber, and Tug McGraw.

In 1976 the Phillies finally broke through. With manager Danny Ozark leading the way, they played fantastic, recording the franchise's first 100-plus-win season! They finished 101–61, winning the NL East by nine games! In 1977 they again went 101–61, outpacing a terrific Pirates team by five games! In 1978 the Phils claimed the division for the third straight year, going 90–72 to win by a game and a half! The Phillies had clearly established themselves as one of the best teams in baseball, and with Schmidt and Carlton they had two of the sport's all-time greats.

Despite all of this, each year the Phils stumbled in MLB's best-of-five National League Championship Series. In '76 they lost to the Reds 3–0, and in both '77 and '78 they lost to the Dodgers 3–1. Fans were extremely frustrated by the playoff defeats, but remained hopeful that perhaps in the coming years the Phillies would win the franchise's first championship.

1980: The Phillies Finally Win the World Series

ENTERING THE 1980 SEASON THE PHILLIES HAD PLAYED BASEBALL for 97 years, but had still not won the World Series. Can you imagine being a 97-year-old person at the start of 1980 knowing your favorite team had not won a title in your lifetime?! Incredibly, until 1980 the Phillies had reached the World Series only twice. In 1915 the Phils lost the World Series to Babe Ruth and the Boston Red Sox 4–1 . In 1950 they lost the World Series to Joe DiMaggio and the New York Yankees 4–0.

With their success of three straight division crowns in the 1970s the Phils had one of the best teams in baseball, but they did not yet have enough. Hoping to improve the club after the '78 season, owner Ruly Carpenter signed superstar Pete Rose to a massive free-agent contract.

Fans were pumped! Rose had won two World Series with the Reds, and he wanted to bring that type of success to Philly.

After a disappointing '79 season in which the Phils failed to make the playoffs, fans wondered if GM Paul Owens would break up the team if they did not make a big run in '80. The club still had major star power with Rose, Mike Schmidt, and Steve Carlton, and they also had a passionate group that included standouts Greg Luzinski, Larry Bowa, Garry Maddox, Bob Boone, Bake McBride, Manny Trillo, Dick Ruthven, and Tug McGraw. However, the Phils let fans down with their play through most of the regular season. But manager Dallas Green, one of the most intense figures ever in Philly sports, kept pushing the club very hard, and in September they got hot, winning 19 of 29 games. They followed that up by winning their first three games in October. Then, in the second-to-last regular season game in a critical matchup versus Montreal, Schmidt, on his way to winning the NL MVP Award, "buried" a home run deep over the left-field wall giving the Phillies the lead in the 11th inning! They held on to win the game and clinch the NL East in dramatic fashion!

Next up was the best-of-five NLCS versus the Astros. It was a wild series, with four of the five games going into extra innings! Many people still believe it is the best playoff series ever played! Trailing 2–1 in games, in Game 4 the Phils rallied from a 2–0 deficit in the eighth inning, and then took the lead for good in the 10th on a huge double by Luzinski which scored Rose from first base as "Charlie Hustle" smashed into catcher Bruce Bochy at home plate! With the series tied 2–2, the Phillies faced future Hall of Famer Nolan Ryan in Game 5. The Phils trailed 5–2 entering the eighth inning, but they battled back again with a dramatic rally to tie it on Del Unser's two-out, pinch-hit single. Then Trillo drove in two more runs with a triple down the left-field line, giving the Phils a 7–5 lead! Unfortunately, the Astros responded, scoring two runs to tie the game 7–7. In the top of the 10th, Maddox hit an RBI single, scoring Unser to give the Phils an 8–7 lead! In the bottom of the 10th, Ruthven retired the final Astros batter on a fly ball to Maddox to end the game!

Tug McGraw (No. 45) and Mike Schmidt (No. 20) celebrate as the Phillies finally win the World Series. (AP Images)

Phillies fans rejoiced knowing the Phils were headed to the World Series for just the third time in franchise history!

The Phillies got off to a quick start in the 1980 World Series, winning the first two games at Veterans Stadium to take a 2–0 series lead! But as the series shifted to Kansas City, things turned bad as KC won the next two. In Game 5 the Phils trailed 3–2 heading into the ninth inning, but they staged another great rally, tying the game on Unser's pinch-hit double, and took the lead on Trillo's RBI single! The Phils held on in the bottom of the ninth to take a 3–2 series lead! They were headed back to Philly needing to win only one more for the first championship in team history!

On **Tuesday, October 21, 1980,** in front of a rabid crowd at Veterans Stadium, the Phils turned to Carlton to pitch the team to glory. In the third inning, Schmidt's single scored two runners, giving the Phils a 2–0 lead! The Phillies continued to battle and took a 4–1 lead into the ninth inning. Dallas Green gave the ball to his excellent closer Tug McGraw to finish off the Royals, but with "The Tugger" on the mound Kansas City threatened in the ninth by loading the bases with one out. In an unusual twist, Royals batter Frank White popped the ball up in foul territory. It looked like catcher Bob Boone would catch it, but when he accidentally dropped the ball, Rose, the first baseman, was standing right there, so Rose caught the deflected ball for the second out! Now the Phillies were just one out away from winning the title! With 97 years of frustration in the past, fans were standing on their feet cheering as Tugger got set to face Royals batter Willie Wilson. After getting ahead of Wilson 1–2 in the count, McGraw went into his wind-up and threw a fastball … and Wilson swung and missed for the final out! Fans were filled with pure joy as the Phillies *finally*, in their 98th season, had won the World Series!

Because it took almost 100 years for the Phils to win the title, some consider the 1980 World Series championship to be Philly's greatest sports moment ever!

Pete Rose (left) and manager Dallas Green (right) helped push the Phillies over the top in 1980. (Bettmann /AP Images)

Wheeze Kids Make One More Push in 1983

FOLLOWING THEIR TITLE IN 1980, the Phils made the playoffs again in '81 but lost early in the postseason. In '82 they missed the playoffs. Entering '83 the window to succeed was shrinking. Gone were classic Phils Greg Luzinski, Larry Bowa, Bob Boone, Manny Trillo, Bake McBride, and Dick Ruthven. In were hitters Von Hayes, Gary Matthews, Bo Díaz, and Iván de Jesús, and pitchers John Denny, Charles Hudson, Kevin Gross, Willie Hernández, and Al Holland. The Phils still had stars Mike Schmidt, Steve Carlton, and Pete Rose, plus Garry Maddox and Tug McGraw. GM Paul Owens also added future Hall of Famers Tony Pérez and Joe Morgan, two of Rose's old teammates from Cincinnati's "Big Red Machine," a squad which had dominated in the 1970s. This meant Rose (42 in April 1983), Pérez (41 in May 1983), and Morgan (40 in September 1983), three of the oldest MLB players, would be on the same team again. Remembering that in 1950 fans called the young Phils "The Whiz Kids," in 1983 fans started calling the old Phils "The Wheeze Kids."

This was a very strange season. The mix of so many old, historically great players created an odd dynamic, and even though the 43–42 Phils were tied for first place in July, the club fired manager Pat Corrales. GM Paul Owens became the manager. Throughout the year Schmidt carried the offense as usual, posting 40 home runs and 109 RBIs! Denny, pitching the best in his career, went 19–6 with a 2.37 ERA on his way to winning the Cy Young Award! The Phils, only 67–64 through August, got hot in September going 22–7 to finish 90–72! They won the NL East by six games!

In the NLCS the Phils faced the Dodgers, who had beaten them 11 of 12 times in the regular season while the Phillies scored only 15 runs in 12 games. But in the NLCS that did not matter as the Phils won two of the first three games in the best-of-five series. In the first inning of Game 4, "The Sarge" (Gary Matthews) hit a shot over the wall, electrifying the Vet crowd with a three-run homer! The Phils carried a 7–2 lead into the ninth inning, when Holland, the closer known as "Mr. T," struck out Bill Russell, thrilling fans and sending The Wheeze Kids to the World Series!

After a Game 1 victory in the Fall Classic, the Phils lost the 1983 World Series in five games to Baltimore. Nevertheless, with the Wheeze Kids having made a push for glory, 1983 was one of the strangest and best years in Phillies history!

Mike Schmidt Hits His 500th Home Run

IN THE LONG HISTORY OF BASEBALL certain career numbers have represented true greatness: 300 wins for a pitcher, 3,000 hits for a batter, and 500 home runs for a slugger stand out. When Mike Schmidt started playing with the Phillies in 1972 only 11 players had ever hit 500 home runs, and no one had done it with the Phils.

In his rookie year of 1973 Schmidt struggled with a .196 batting average. He did hit 18 homers though, giving fans some hope he could become good. In 1974 he had his first excellent season, leading the NL with 36 home runs. He followed that up with 38 homers each of the next two seasons, and in 1976 Schmidt led the Phillies to the postseason for the first time since 1950! He even hit four home runs in one game that year! With Schmidt starring the Phils made the playoffs in '76, '77, and '78. In the Phillies World Series winning year of 1980, he had a spectacular season with career highs of 48 home runs and 121 RBIs! He won the National League Gold Glove at third base and the NL MVP Award! He was also the MVP of the World Series! "Schmidty" was a baseball superstar. After 1980, Schmidt remained remarkably consistent with season home run totals of 31, 35, 40, 36, 33, and 37. When the 1987 season started he was just five home runs short of 500. Halfway through April he had hit four more, bringing his total to 499.

With a chance to make history, Schmidt did so in dramatic fashion. Trailing Pittsburgh 6–5 in the ninth inning, with two men on base and two outs, legendary announcer Harry Kalas called the action: "Here's the stretch by Robinson ... the 3–0 pitch .... Swing and a long drive!... There it is!... Number 500!... The career 500th home run for Michael Jack Schmidt!... And the Phillies have regained the lead in Pittsburgh 8–6!... And the Phillies dugout comes swarming out to home plate!" Schmidt rounded the bases with great joy as Phils fans everywhere celebrated!

The greatest Phillies player, Mike Schmidt, hits his 500th home run in Pittsburgh. (George Gojkovich/Getty Images)

Two years later Schmidt finished his career with an awesome 548 home runs, eight NL home run titles, three MVPs, and 10 Gold Gloves! He was also a 12-time All-Star who helped the Phils reach the playoffs six times, and along the way established himself as the best Phillies player ever and as the greatest third baseman in baseball history! Schmidt was inducted into the Baseball Hall of Fame in 1995!

'93 Phils Go from Worst to First

AFTER GETTING BACK TO THE WORLD SERIES IN 1983, the Phillies fell on hard times. Beginning in '84 they played a lot of bad baseball. Fans suffered as the club struggled. From 1984 to 1992 the Phils had only one season above .500. In '92 the Phillies were particularly terrible, finishing last in the NL East. But in 1993 owner Bill Giles and the rest of the organization were determined to turn things around, and with stars Lenny Dykstra, Darren Daulton, and John Kruk, that is exactly what they did. GM Lee Thomas made a lot of off-season moves, adding veteran players. Suddenly the Phils had a quality pitching rotation with Curt Schilling, Tommy Greene, Terry Mulholland, Danny Jackson, and Ben Rivera. Plus, the bullpen was strong with Larry Andersen, David West, and closer Mitch "Wild Thing" Williams. The Phils also had a solid collection of position players such as Dave Hollins, Mickey Morandini, Mariano Duncan, Wes Chamberlain, Jim Eisenreich, Pete Incaviglia, Milt Thompson, and Ricky Jordan. It was up to manager Jim Fregosi to put it all together while getting assistance from pitching coach Johnny Podres.

The Phillies started off hot in April sweeping the Astros, and winning eight of their first nine games. From there the Phils raced out to a 45–17 record with a very strong hold on first place! Fans loved the Phillies excellent brand of baseball, their rough and tumble "Macho Row" style, and their wacky personalities. Fans also loved the crazy ways that the

'93 Phils won games. There was a comeback from an 8–0 hole to beat the Giants; Thompson's game-saving catch in San Diego preventing a grand slam; Morandini's tremendous defensive double-play in the bottom of the ninth in LA; Duncan's grand slam off of Lee Smith on Mother's Day; a 20-inning win on a hit by Dykstra; a victory at 4:40 AM on a base hit by relief pitcher Mitch Williams; and a grand slam by Kim Batiste to win a game in the bottom of the ninth! On and on and on the thrills went! It was a magical season. Fans were crazy for the '93 Phils!

In July, the club got stronger with the addition of rookie Kevin Stocker as the team's new starting shortstop. Through it all, "Dutch" Daulton was the team's leader, and Dykstra, who hit .305 with 19 home runs while scoring an awesome 143 runs, was the club's best player. In mid-September the Phillies held off Montreal, and in late September they beat Pittsburgh to win the NL East for the first time in 10 years! It was party time for a team that had not been expected to reach the playoffs!

The Phils finished the regular season 97–65 for the then third-best record in club history! Next was the National League Championship Series against a tremendous Atlanta Braves team that had won an amazing 104 regular season games. Atlanta had a very strong lineup and one of the best pitching staffs in baseball history. With future Hall of Fame pitchers Greg Maddux, Tom Glavine, and John Smoltz, plus the outstanding Steve Avery, most people in America thought the Phils had little shot to beat Atlanta. Schilling started the series off in Game 1 setting a playoff record by striking out the first five Braves batters he faced! Batiste, who had made a costly throwing error in the top of the ninth, was the hero in extra innings with an RBI single, giving the Phils the Game 1 victory! The Phillies dropped the next two games, but then in Atlanta in one of the most important starts of the season, Danny Jackson pitched a truly gutsy game as the Phils won Game 4 to even the series up 2–2! In Game 5 Schilling was masterful, shutting out Atlanta through eight innings, and then Dykstra hit one of the biggest homers in club history as the Phils won in extra innings to take a 3–2 series lead!

Now all eyes turned to Veterans Stadium for Game 6. Fans were rocking in the stands as the Phils were one win away from advancing

Darren Daulton (standing) embraces Mitch Williams as the Phillies celebrate defeating the Atlanta Braves in Game 6 of the 1993 National League Championship Series. (Tom Mihalek/Getty Images)

to the World Series. The Braves were sending NL Cy Young Award winner Maddux to the mound; the Phillies were starting Tommy Greene. Daulton got the scoring going with a two-run RBI double! Hollins hit a two-run home run, and then Morandini ripped a two-run triple! Greene held the Braves down as the Phils took a 6–3 lead into the ninth inning. With the Vet crowd in an absolute frenzy with excitement, Mitch Williams retired Atlanta by striking out Bill Pecota for the final out, setting off an awesome celebration! The Wild Thing jumped high in the air, Daulton ran to hug him, and the entire Phillies team rushed to celebrate together! The '93 Phils had defeated Atlanta to win the National League pennant! Fans at the Vet and all around the Delaware Valley celebrated as the Phils were headed to the World Series!

Unfortunately, the Phillies lost a hard-fought World Series in six games to the Toronto Blue Jays in heartbreaking fashion. Nevertheless, the '93 Phils will always be beloved for their skill, wacky personality, all-out effort, incredible ways of winning, and their connection to fans. They provided so much joy during a thrilling season. Few teams, if any, have ever had a greater bond with Philadelphia sports fans!

Back-to-Back MVPs, "the Team to Beat," and Overcoming Seven Down with 17 to Go

FOLLOWING 1993, THE PHILS RETURNED TO THEIR LOSING WAYS. In the late '90s they had stars Curt Schilling, Scott Rolen, and Bobby Abreu; still, the club did not finish above .500 from 1994 to 2000. When they did climb above .500 in '01, '03, '04, and '05, the Phils just were not good enough as they always missed the playoffs. GM Ed Wade and assistant GMs Rubén Amaro and Mike Arbuckle developed quality young prospects, and star Jim Thome provided thrills, but fans were very frustrated. However, in the mid-2000s, hope picked up as the Phils built their team around the tremendous talents of Ryan Howard, Chase Utley, Jimmy Rollins, and pitcher Cole Hamels. Howard and Rollins led the way in '06 and '07, as the duo accomplished the rare feat of teammates winning back-to-back MVPs!

Howard's '06 season is amongst the best anyone has ever had in Philly sports. Coming off winning the Rookie of the Year Award in '05, expectations were high for the Phils new slugger. In April Howard hit five home runs. In May he got hot with 13 homers! In June he hit nine more, so halfway through the season his total was 27! In July Howard hit nine more! Then his 14 homers in August moved him past Mike Schmidt's team record of 48 in a season! On September 22 he connected for his final homer of the year, raising his total to 58! Howard was incredible! With 58 home runs, 149 RBIs, a .313 batting average, a .425 on-base percentage, and a .659 slugging percentage, "the Big Piece" won the NL MVP!

Despite Howard's success, the Phils missed the playoffs again. In the off-season, Rollins wanted to jump-start the club for '07. Talking to reporters, he said, "I think we are the team to beat in the NL East." It was bold and shocking, and it put a target on Rollins and the Phils. But in '07 "J-Roll" handled all the pressure. He dominated with speed and power on offense while playing spectacular defense at shortstop, winning his first Gold Glove! Rollins stats were awesome: a .296 average, 30 home runs, 94 RBIs, 139 runs scored, 41 stolen bases, 38 doubles, and 20 triples! Most importantly, with fans desperate to see the Phils make the playoffs, he led them as they rallied from seven games back of the Mets with just 17 games left to play! On the regular season's last day the Phillies delivered on J-Roll's declaration as Brett Myers closed out the Nationals in thrilling fashion at Citizens Bank Park to win the NL East! Proving they had been "the team to beat," the Phils advanced to the playoffs for the first time in 14 seasons! Despite losing in the postseason, hope was high that Howard, Rollins, Utley, Hamels, and others might soon win a championship for Philly.

Ryan Howard (left) and Jimmy Rollins (right) won back-to-back MVP Awards and helped the Phils capture the World Series in 2008. (Tom Mihalek/AP Images)

The Championship Drought Is Over; Phillies Win the 2008 World Series

AT THE START OF THE 2008 BASEBALL SEASON none of Philly's four main teams (Phillies, Flyers, Sixers, and Eagles) had won a championship since the Sixers won the title in 1983. It had been 25 years—25 very, very long years—and fans were starving for a winner. But under the leadership of owner David Montgomery, the Phils had improved, and coming off their '07 postseason trip with stars Ryan Howard, Chase Utley, Jimmy Rollins, and Cole Hamels, the Phillies seemed poised for greatness.

Prior to the 2008 season general manager Pat Gillick acquired closer Brad Lidge to improve the bullpen. The roster also included key players such as Pat Burrell, Shane Victorino, Jayson Werth, Carlos Ruiz, Pedro Feliz, Brett Myers, Jamie Moyer, Ryan Madson, and J.C. Romero. Despite all this talent, the Phils did not live up to expectations for most of the regular season. In mid-August they were only 64–57. Fans were disappointed. But similar to 1980 when the Phillies got hot down the stretch, the '08 squad started playing better ball under manager Charlie Manuel. In their final 16 regular season games the Phillies went 13–3, and on the second-to-last day of the regular season they won the NL East as Rollins, Utley, and Howard turned an amazing double play to secure the game! Lidge earned the save, finishing the regular season a perfect 41-for-41 in save opportunities!

In the National League Divisional Series the Phillies faced the Milwaukee Brewers. The Phils won Game 1. In Game 2 Victorino hit a dramatic grand slam off of Brewers star pitcher C.C. Sabathia, helping to give the Phils a 2–0 series lead! They dropped Game 3, but rebounded in Game 4 as Rollins led off the game off with a home run, and the Phils cruised to victory, winning the series 3–1!

Next the Phillies faced Manny Ramirez and the red-hot Los Angeles Dodgers. Again the Phillies took a 2–0 series lead, and again they dropped Game 3 on the road. In Game 4, in one of the most pivotal moments of the playoffs, Victorino hit an eighth-inning home run to tie the game, and then Matt Stairs hit a two-run homer "deep into the night" giving the Phillies a 7–5 lead! The Phils won Game 4 to take a 3–1 series lead! In Game 5 Rollins again got the Phils going right away with a lead-off home run to start the game, and Hamels controlled LA's bats throughout as the Phils advanced to the World Series for just the sixth time in franchise history!

Next up was the Tampa Bay Rays in the World Series. In Game 1 Utley hit a first-inning homer, and Hamels, on his way to winning the World Series MVP Award, once again pitched very well to give the Phils a 1–0 series lead! Game 2 was tough as starting pitcher Brett Myers struggled, and the series was evened up 1–1. In Game 3 the Phillies won as Ruiz got the winning hit with an RBI infield single in the bottom of the ninth inning, giving the Phils a 2–1 series lead! In Game 4 the Phillies bats exploded for 10 runs, including two home runs from Ryan Howard and a homer from pitcher Joe Blanton, as they took a 3–1 series lead! Now all eyes turned to Hamels for Game 5.

Game 5 of the 2008 World Series was not only one of the strangest games in Philadelphia sports history, it was one of the strangest games in all of sports history. It rained so much during Game 5 that the umpires almost called the game due to rain with the Phillies leading after the fifth inning. Had that happened, the Phils potentially could have claimed to have won the World Seires due to rain stopping the game after the fifth inning with the Phillies in the lead. But before the umpires stopped the action, Tampa Bay scored a run in the sixth inning to tie it, so when the umpires suspended the game for the night due to rain it was tied 2–2.

Two days later when it stopped raining on **October 29, 2008,** the game resumed as fans wondered if this would be the night the Phillies would finally end the city's championship drought. In the top of the seventh inning Utley, one of the best, most instinctive Phils players ever, helped the cause by making a spectacular defensive play. He threw a Rays runner out at home plate to end the inning while keeping it a 3–3 score! In the bottom of the seventh Feliz singled home Eric Bruntlett giving the Phils a 4–3 lead! After getting through the eighth with no change in the score, it was up to Lidge in the ninth. With two outs and a runner on second base he faced pinch-hitter Eric Hinske. Fans at Citizens Bank Park were going absolutely wild with anticipation. The great Phillies announcer, Harry Kalas, called the action for 1210-AM: "Fans on their feet … rally towels are being waived … Brad Lidge stretches … the 0–2 pitch … swing and a miss! Struck him out! The Philadelphia Phillies are 2008 World Champions of Baseball! Brad Lidge does it again, and stays perfect for the 2008 season! 48-for-48 in save opportunities! And let this city celebrate!" And celebrate the fans did, with one of the most jubilant explosions of happiness in our town's history! Philadelphia *finally* after 25 years was once again a champion!

Shane Victorino (No. 8), the Flyin' Hawaiian, leaps on the pile as the Phillies celebrate winning the World Series in 2008. (Jeff Zelevansky/Getty Images)

Roy Halladay's Amazing Season

FOLLOWING THEIR CHAMPIONSHIP SEASON IN 2008, the Phils had another great team in 2009. The '09 club provided thrilling moments such as Jimmy Rollins' double off of LA pitcher Jonathan Broxton to win Game 4 of the NLCS, and Cliff Lee's masterful performance in Game 1 of the Fall Classic! Unfortunately, the Phils lost the 2009 World Series to Derek Jeter, Alex Rodriguez, and the New York Yankees. Looking to improve in 2010, Phils GM Rubén Amaro traded for Toronto's star pitcher, Roy Halladay. He had excelled in the American League for years, but Toronto had not been great, so Halladay had never pitched in a postseason game. He and the Phillies hoped that would change with "Doc" Halladay now pitching for the Phils.

In his first year in Philly, Halladay had a historic season. He won on Opening Day, and dominated in his next three starts, improving his record to 4–0. In late May versus the Marlins, Halladay pitched the best game of his life by throwing a perfect game! He retired all 27 batters he faced without allowing a hit, a walk, or anyone to reach base at all! It was just the second perfect game in Phillies history, and only the 20th in Major League Baseball history!

Throughout the summer Halladay continued to excel. In September he won four straight starts, and then on September 27 he pitched a complete game two-hit shutout in Washington to help the Phillies clinch their fourth consecutive National League East crown! On his way to winning the NL Cy Young Award, Halladay finished the regular season with a 21–10 record, nine complete games, four shutouts, 219 strikeouts, and an awesome 2.44 ERA!

In Game 1 of the NLCS he made his playoff debut against Cincinnati. Incredibly, Halladay pitched a no-hitter! Catcher Carlos Ruiz made a terrific play for the final out by throwing the ball from his knees to Ryan Howard at first base! This was just the second no-hitter in playoff history! Halladay accomplished something no one else had ever done by pitching a perfect game in the regular season and a no-hitter in the postseason! He truly had one of the great seasons in Philly sports history!

Tragically, Halladay died in a plane crash in 2017. He was inducted after his death into the Baseball Hall of Fame in 2019.

Roy Halladay (right) and Carlos Ruiz (left) hug after Halladay's playoff no-hitter. (Matt Slocum/AP Images)

2022 Phillies Bring Red October Back to Citizens Bank Park

THE PHILLIES RUN OF EXCELLENCE with core players Ryan Howard, Chase Utley, Jimmy Rollins, and Cole Hamels ended at the conclusion of the 2011 season. That year had been a particularly special regular season as the Phils won a club record 102 games and, for the first time in franchise history, captured the NL East for the fifth straight year! However, after losing in the playoffs the Phils went backward quickly. Injuries and age set in. Fans were extremely upset as the team missed the playoffs for the next 10 years.

Entering the 2022 season, expectations had risen, but fans still had doubts despite an improved roster. Through the years, Aaron Nola, Rhys Hoskins, Seranthony Domínguez, Ranger Suárez, Alec Bohm, and Bryson Stott emerged from the farm system; J.T. Realmuto, Jean Segura, and José Alvarado had been acquired in trades; and with the massive spending of owner John Middleton, the Phils signed free-agent star Bryce Harper, Zack Wheeler, Kyle Schwarber, and Nick Castellanos. Harper was awesome in 2021, winning the NL MVP Award when he hit .309 with a .429 on-base percentage and a .615 slugging percentage while mashing 35 home runs! Nevertheless, with so much disappointment in recent years of the Phillies missing the playoffs, fans wondered why 2022 would be any different.

For two months things were not different. The 2022 Phils started a brutal 22–29 under manager Joe Girardi. On June 2, Middleton and president of baseball operations Dave Dombrowski fired Girardi. Rob Thomson was named manager. Then the Phils got real hot. In June they went 19–8. In July, 15–10. In August, 18–11. Entering September the Phillies had a good chance to claim one of the three NL Wild Card spots, but two five-game losing streaks, including one in late September, hurt their chances. Fortunately, after the second losing streak the team rallied, winning three of its next four, setting up a game in Houston in which the club's longest tenured player, Nola, could pitch them into the postseason. Pitching 6⅔ no-hit innings, Nola was exceptional before turning it over to the bullpen. In the ninth Zach Eflin recorded the final out, sending the Phils back to the postseason for the first time since 2011! Players erupted in celebration, and TV coverage showed them in the clubhouse demonstrating more personality than the public had seen before as Rob Thomson popped champagne to toast his club! The Phils blasted their theme song, "Dancing On My Own," as they headed to the playoffs!

In the Wild Card round the Phils faced the Cardinals in a best-of-three series in St. Louis. Game 1 was rough for a while as the Phils bats struggled, but in the top of the ninth, down 2–0, the Phils scored six runs, which included a huge two-run single by Segura helping the Phils win! In Game 2 Nola was masterful, and the Phils beat the Cards to advance to the next round! As the club celebrated in a road locker room again, fans were now fully on-board! This team was fun, good, and likeable.

In the NLDS the Phillies faced the Braves in a best-of-five series. Again the series started on the road. After splitting the first two games, the Phils came home to Citizens Bank Park in front of rabid fans excited for the return of Red October to Philly! In Game 3, facing Spencer Strider, Hoskins, who had been struggling, hit a shot for a three-run home run! Citizens Bank Park went wild as Hoskins slammed his bat to the ground with joy! The Phils won Game 3 and Game 4 to advance to the National League Championship Series for the first time since 2010!

In the NLCS the Phils faced the Padres in a best-of-seven series, and after splitting the first two, the Phils won Game 3 and 4, taking a 3–1 series lead! In the eighth inning of Game 5, while trailing 3–2, announcer Scott Franzke called the action on SportsRadio 94WIP as Harper batted: "Two balls, two strikes to Bryce Harper … Suárez delivers … swing and a drive … left field … it's deep … it's going … and it is gone! It is Bedlam at the Bank as Bryce Harper has put the Phillies on top!" Fans roared with excitement, amazed and thrilled with what

Bryce Harper connects in Game 5 of the 2022 National League Championship Series setting off Bedlam at the Bank. (Matt Rourke/AP Images)

Harper had just done! Everyone immediately knew this was one of the biggest moments in Phillies history!

Then in the ninth Ranger Suárez shut down San Diego as Castellanos caught the final out, sending the Phils to the World Series for the first time in 13 years! With years of immense frustration behind them, fans were now full of so much joy!

After tremendous victories in Game 1 and Game 3 of the Fall Classic, the Phils lost a hard-fought World Series in six games to Houston. However, in showing their grit, talent, and personality while connecting with each other and with fans, the 2022 Phils reignited a love affair between the club and its fans! Red October established hope that perhaps in the coming years this group, like '80 and '08, could win it all.

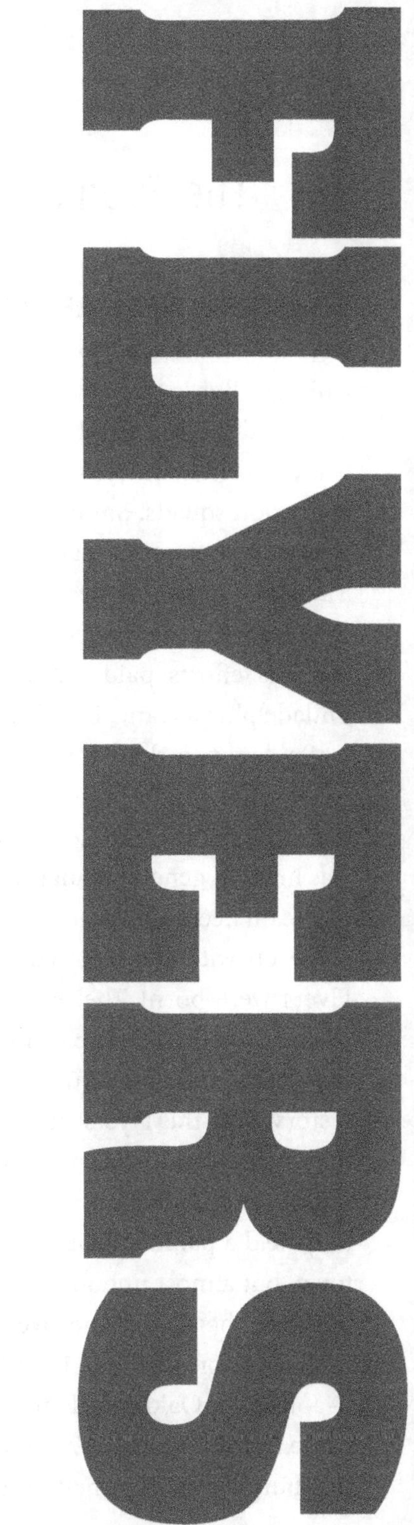
FLYERS

The Founding of the Organization

THE NATIONAL HOCKEY LEAGUE BEGAN IN 1917, and for many years there were only six clubs: Montreal, Toronto, Boston, New York, Detroit, and Chicago. But in the 1960s NHL owners wanted to expand the league, so they decided to add six new teams. When businessman Ed Snider heard this news he jumped at the chance to get Philly one of the NHL's expansion squads. Snider was a part-owner of the Eagles, but he loved hockey ever since he saw the Rangers and Canadiens play a game at Madison Square Garden earlier in his life. Snider applied to the NHL for a franchise, and began raising $2 million for the league's expansion fee. His efforts paid off. On February 9, 1966, the NHL awarded Philadelphia a team. The NHL was coming to Philly!

Snider knew there was a lot of work to be done. They needed a home, so he set out to build the Spectrum, a hockey and basketball arena in South Philly. He also needed to put together a hockey staff. Bud Poile was hired as general manager, and Keith Allen was hired as head coach. The team needed a name, so a contest was held for fans to see who could come up with the best name. "Flyers" was chosen. The Philadelphia Flyers were born! The organization needed players, so they selected them in the NHL's Expansion Draft. Future Hall of Fame goaltender Bernie Parent, who would become one of the greatest players in team history, was the Flyers first pick. They also needed an announcer, so they hired Gene Hart to broadcast games. Hart helped build a very important connection with fans. Right before the Flyers first season they held a parade through Philly to showcase the new players around town, but almost nobody showed up to watch. The team would have to prove on the ice that they were worthy of people's attention.

Finally, on October 11, 1967, the Flyers played their first game, a 5–1 loss in Oakland. Eight days later they played their first home game in front of about 7,800 fans. The Flyers won that game, defeating Pittsburgh 1–0. That first-season crowd size at home games increased as the Orange and Black went a respectable 31–32–11 to win their division. Philadelphia was starting to take an interest in the Flyers. As the club improved over the next few years, a love affair took off. Fans became intensely passionate about the Flyers as they got set to dominate the NHL.

Flyers Win the Stanley Cup in 1974 and 1975

PERHAPS NO TEAM HAS EVER BEEN MORE IDENTIFIED with Philadelphia than the Flyers Stanley Cup–winning squads of 1973–74 and '74–75. Tough, gutsy, blue-collar, and hard-working, these Flyers teams were phenomenal, and they formed a special bond with Philly sports fans. Led by captain Bobby Clarke, they played an extremely aggressive style of hockey, intimidating opponents and often fighting them. "The Broad Street Bullies," as the Flyers were called, angered opposing teams and fans from other cities who thought the Flyers were unsportsmanlike. But with owner Ed Snider, GM Keith Allen, and coach Fred Shero leading the way, the Flyers did not care what others thought about them. They were going to play their style of hockey, and everyone else was just going to have to deal with it.

It would not be easy for the Flyers to rise to glory. As an expansion team in 1967, they were way behind the best teams in the league. The Flyers took their lumps in the early years, but learned from it and added talent along the way. Clarke arrived in their third year in 1969. People questioned whether he could be good in the NHL because he was diabetic, but the captain proved doubters wrong. He became a three-time league MVP and the player most often considered the best in Flyers history! Goalie Bernie Parent was the club's first pick in the 1967 Expansion Draft, but the Flyers traded him in '71 and then reacquired him in '73. "Only God saves more than Bernie" was the popular saying because of how elite he was at stopping the puck. Bernie became a two-time Vezina Trophy winner as the NHL's top goalie! Forward Bill Barber was another huge addition in the '72 Draft. Barber went on to set the Flyers record for most goals scored! All three players eventually were inducted into the Hockey Hall of Fame! The team also had enforcers. "The Hammer," Dave Shultz (820 penalty minutes in two Cup seasons), and "The Hound," Bob Kelly, fought opponents to protect Clarke and others! Plus Rick MacLeish, Jim Watson, Joe Watson, Ross Lonsberry, and Gary Dornhoefer were key players as well.

Despite their talent, it seemed unlikely the Flyers would win the Stanley Cup in '74 because it was just their seventh year as a franchise. Expansion teams do not usually win a title so fast. But the Flyers had a fantastic regular season, going 50–16–12! Then in the playoffs they beat the Atlanta Flames and the New York Rangers to advance to the Stanley

Bobby Clarke leaps with joy upon scoring perhaps the most important goal in Flyers history, an overtime winner in Game 2 of the 1974 Stanley Cup Final. (AP Images)

Cup Finals, where they would face the mighty Bobby Orr and the Boston Bruins! The Flyers dropped Game 1, but in overtime of Game 2 Clarke scored one of the most important goals in franchise history to even the series 1–1! The Flyers then won two in row before Boston won Game 5, making it a 3–2 series.

This all set up Game 6 at the Spectrum on **May 19, 1974,** as the Flyers took the ice with a chance to capture Lord Stanley's Cup in front of their fans. Prior to the game, Shero told his team, "Win today, and we walk together forever." The Flyers also had a special good luck charm (perhaps the best good luck charm in sports) in famed singer Kate Smith. Up until that point when she sang "God Bless America" live in person or with a pre-recorded version before games the Orange and Black's record was an unbelievable 36–3–1! Flyers winger Rick MacLeish got the scoring going as he tallied a first-period goal for a 1–0 lead! That was all Bernie would need as he controlled the action throughout the game, stopping all 30 Bruins shots! Late in the third period with the Flyers still leading 1–0, the Spectrum crowd was going wild with excitement as the clock ticked down. Legendary announcer Gene Hart called the action on WTAF: "Fifteen seconds left in the game … 10 seconds … Orr shoots it down the ice … Parent makes the save.… Ladies and gentlemen, the Flyers are going to win the Stanley Cup! The Flyers win the Stanley Cup! The Flyers win the Stanley Cup! The Flyers have won the Stanley Cup!" Yes, they had, and in just their seventh year! The next day about 2 million fans continued to celebrate as a parade was held on Broad Street for the Broad Street Bullies!

With one championship in hand, the Flyers came back in '74–75 hungry for more, acquiring winger Reggie Leach to form the "LCB Line": Leach, Clarke, and Barber. The Flyers had another great regular season, going 51–18–11! In the playoffs they beat Toronto 4–0 in the first round, and then defeated the Islanders in seven games to reach the Finals again! After splitting the first four Cup games, the Flyers won Game 5! Then in Game 6 on **May 27, 1975,** in Buffalo, Kelly and Bill Clement each scored, and Bernie shut out the Sabres, leading the Flyers to another Stanley Cup title! For the second straight year Bernie won the

Bobby Clarke (left) and Bernie Parent (right), the two greatest Flyers, skate with the Stanley Cup in 1974. (Bruce Bennett/Getty Images)

Conn Smythe Trophy as playoff MVP! Incredibly, including the regular season and postseason, he had 30 shutouts over two seasons! The Flyers, the expansion team few gave any chance to win in their early years, had won back-to-back Stanley Cup titles, and in the process captured the hearts of Philly sports fans!

America Is Proud as the Flyers Defeat the Soviet Red Army Team

THROUGHOUT THE LATE 1940s, '50s, '60s, '70s, AND '80s, the United States and the Soviet Union, the world's other superpower, squared off in a dangerous stand-off that was known as "The Cold War." While not directly engaged in war, the US and USSR did not like each other. Both nations had the capability to cause tremendous damage to the other country if they attacked with nuclear weapons.

Such was the backdrop of hostilities in 1976 as the Flyers took center stage in perhaps the most unique game ever in Philadelphia sports. The United States and the Soviet Union had agreed to allow hockey to be on the frontline of commerce between the two nations, with a series of games featuring select NHL teams against one of two Soviet squads, including their famed Red Army team. Most people believed the Soviet Red Army team was the greatest in the world. They crushed the Rangers 7–3, beat Boston 5–2, and tied the Canadiens. As the series of games was coming to a close, one more game remained: the Soviet Red Army team versus the Flyers, winners of back-to-back Stanley Cups, in an internationally televised matchup from the Spectrum. It was a rare opportunity for the Flyers, as they were in a sense representing the NHL and the entire United States.

The game was fierce from the start, as the Flyers played their usual rough and tumble style of hard-hitting hockey, frustrating and inflicting pain on the Soviets. Flyers defenseman Ed Van Impe hit Soviet star Valeri Kharlamov so hard he stayed down on the ice for over a minute. The Soviet coach decided he had seen enough; he ordered his team off the ice in protest of the Broad Street Bullies style of hockey! Flyers owner Ed Snider yelled at Soviet officials, telling them that if the Red Army team did not continue playing they would not be paid any money for their North American trip. After 17 minutes of protest, the Soviets decided to resume the game, and when they did the Flyers dominated. First, Reggie Leach scored! Then, Rick MacLeish made it 2–0! Joe Watson scored the third straight Flyers goal! When it was all over, the Flyers had outshot the Soviets 49–13 for a thrilling 4–1 victory! The Orange and Black had stood up to the Soviet Red Army team, breaking their will and defeating them, and in the process made fans all across America very proud of the Philadelphia Flyers!

Reggie Leach Sets a Franchise Record for Goals in a Season

AFTER WINNING THE CLUB'S FIRST STANLEY CUP IN 1974, the Flyers found a way to upgrade the following season with the addition of scoring sensation Reggie Leach. Leach, a right wing forward, joined Bobby Clarke and Bill Barber to form one of the greatest lines ever assembled in hockey, the "LCB Line." Leach, Clarke, and Barber had tremendous skill and chemistry together. In his first season with the Flyers, Leach tallied 45 goals and 33 assists for 78 regular season points, helping Clarke, Barber, Bernie Parent, and the rest of the Flyers capture their second Stanley Cup!

The following season in 1975–76 Leach turned in perhaps the most spectacular individual season by a forward in the history of the franchise. Playing in 80 regular season games, he tallied an awesome 61 goals, which still stands to this day as the club record for most goals by a Flyers player in a regular season! At the time, Leach's 61 goals were the fourth most ever scored in an NHL season! Plus, he had 30 assists for 91 overall points. Then in the postseason, Leach continued his historic play. In 16 playoff games he scored 19 more goals, setting an NHL mark for the most goals ever scored in one postseason! Incredibly, Leach's 19 goals still stands as tied for the most goals ever scored in one postseason, despite the fact that he did it in just three rounds of playoff hockey instead of the four-round format that has been used for years since! He also set a postseason record by scoring in 10 straight games! He even scored five goals in one game, as the Flyers defeated the Boston Bruins to advance to the Stanley Cup Finals! It is remarkable that between the regular season and postseason Leach scored 80 goals in one NHL season!

Despite the fact that the Flyers lost the Stanley Cup Finals 4–0 to the Montreal Canadiens, for his amazing efforts in the 1976 playoffs Leach won the Conn Smythe Trophy as the MVP of the postseason. He is one of only six players to ever win the award from the losing team in the Cup Finals. Leach would go on to play six more seasons for the Flyers, tallying a tremendous 306 goals and 208 assists over eight seasons with the Orange and Black! He is certainly one of the best players in franchise history!

Flyers Go 35 Straight Games Unbeaten

IN THE 1979–80 SEASON THE FLYERS ACCOMPLISHED something truly phenomenal. With a talented roster that included longtime stars Bobby Clarke, Bill Barber, Rick MacLeish, and Reggie Leach, plus younger players Ken Linseman, Paul Holmgren, and Brian Propp, the Flyers got on a roll ... a very big role. Sometimes in sports a team gets hot, winning five, six, or seven games in a row, or they get really hot, winning 10 in a row. In the NHL, a league with games that could end in a tie until 2004, a team might get really, really hot with wins and ties leading to an unbeaten streak of 12 or maybe 15 games in a row. But what the Flyers did in '79–80 went way, way, way beyond that, as they went an unbelievable 35 straight games without a loss!

The streak began on October 14, 1979, with a 4–3 win over Toronto. The Flyers then won their next two games before tying Montreal, and then won nine more in a row after that. They had an unbeaten streak of 13 games! Next, they tied St Louis, won two in a row, tied Edmonton, again won two more in a row, rattled off three straight ties, won again, and then tied Chicago on December 9, bringing their unbeaten streak to 24 games! Goaltenders Pete Peeters and Phil Myre were both playing great. The Flyers then won their next two, and then tied two more, upping their streak to 28 games! On December 22, versus Boston, the Flyers won 5–2, setting a new NHL record with 29 straight games without a loss! They followed that up with a win, a tie, and then four more wins in a row, including a 4–2 victory over Buffalo on January 6, 1980, running their streak to 35 consecutive games without a loss! The next day the Flyers finally lost 7–1 to Minnesota ending their streak. They had gone 25–0–10 for an NHL record 60 points in only 35 games!

To put in perspective this accomplishment, the NBA's longest winning streak is 33 games by the Los Angeles Lakers in the 1971–72 season, MLB's longest streak is 26 games by the 1916 New York Giants, and the NFL's longest streak is 21 games by the New England Patriots during the 2003 and 2004 seasons. Of course, the Flyers benefited with ties, but their 35-game unbeaten streak remains the longest in NHL history, and a record sports historians consider almost unbreakable! The Flyers advanced all the way to the Stanley Cup Finals in '80, but lost to the New York Islanders. Still, the streak remains a remarkable achievement of greatness!

Incredible Runs in 1985 and 1987

WHEN THE LEGENDARY BOBBY CLARKE RETIRED IN 1984 to become the club's general manager, the Flyers shaped their roster around a terrific core of Dave Poulin, Tim Kerr, Brian Propp, Mark Howe, and sensational young goalie Pelle Lindbergh. With intense coach Mike Keenan, the 1984–85 Flyers had an excellent season, as Lindbergh won the Vezina Trophy as the NHL's best goaltender. In Game 6 of the Prince of Wales Conference Finals, Poulin scored a rare two-man, shorthanded goal versus Quebec as the Flyers advanced to the Stanley Cup Finals! Unfortunately, they lost to the greatest NHL player ever, Wayne Gretzky, and his amazing Edmonton Oilers 4–1. Tragically, early in the 1985–86 season, Lindbergh died in a car crash. It was shocking and completely devastating to the Flyers and their fans. Despite still being a very good team without Lindbergh, the Flyers lost early in the '86 playoffs.

But in the '86–87 season the Flyers went on another magical run. With rookie goalie Ron Hextall joining the Flyers core, plus contributions from Peter Zezel, Rick Tocchet, Scott Mellanby, Murray Craven, Pelle Eklund, Doug Crossman, Brad McCrimmon, and others, the Flyers passionate play captivated Philly, as they got back to the Finals by beating Montreal! In the close out Game 6 in Montreal, the Flyers and Canadiens got into a huge brawl before the game! Philadelphia loved this team! Once again in the Cup Finals the Flyers would face the mighty Oilers. With Gretzky and other future Hall of Famers such as Mark Messier, Jari Kurri, Paul Coffey, and Grant Fuhr, the Oilers were one of the greatest teams ever in *any* sport. The Oilers skill showed as they won three of the first four games. The Flyers rebounded to win Game 5, but trailed 2–0 in Game 6 before scoring three straight goals, which included Propp's goal to tie it, and J.J. Daigneault's thrilling slap-shot goal giving the Flyers a 3–2 lead! The Spectrum crowd exploded in excitement! Fans continued cheering with joy as the Flyers held on to force a Game 7!

Unfortunately, the Flyers lost Game 7 in Edmonton 3–1. Despite being on the losing team, Hextall was awarded the Conn Smythe Trophy as MVP of the playoffs. It was disappointing to see the Flyers lose the Cup again, but their passionate play, determination, and heart all season inspired fans and continued the tradition of a love affair between Philadelphia and the Flyers!

A Goalie Scores

AT THE START OF THE 1987–88 SEASON NO GOALTENDER had ever scored a goal in an NHL game by shooting the puck into the net. One goalie, Billy Smith of the New York Islanders, had been credited with a goal because he was the last player from his team to touch the puck before the other team accidentally put it into their own net, but it was not like Smith actually scored the goal himself. Ron Hextall, the Flyers fantastic young goalie, was unique because he was extremely athletic, liked to be physical, was willing to fight, and was excellent at handling the puck. Hextall wanted to be the first goalie to truly score.

"Hexy," as he was called, already was a fan-favorite having helped the Flyers advance to the Stanley Cup Finals in '87. Now in his second season, he looked for a chance to make more history. In December against Boston, the Flyers led 4–2 late in the third period when the Bruins pulled their goaltender out of the game to get an extra offensive player on the ice in order to maximize their chance of scoring. Hextall knew the Bruins net was empty. He was looking for an opportunity to score. Legendary Flyers announcer Gene Hart called the action: "Bruins come back … flip it from their side of center in on Hextall … he blocks … looks to shoot it to the open net … he has …… SCORED! Ron Hextall has become the first player in the history of the National Hockey League, the first goaltender to actually score a goal!" Fans at the Spectrum went nuts in celebration, amazed with what they had just seen! Flyers players left the bench to congratulate Hextall on the awesome accomplishment!

Hexy's goal was the first of its kind in the NHL's 71 years! Before he scored, there had been many thousands of games without a goalie actually scoring! Incredibly, the following season Hexy did it again! In Game 5 of a playoff series versus Washington he scored an empty-net goal, becoming the first goalie to ever score in a playoff game! Hextall went on to have a terrific career with the Flyers over two different stints while playing 11 seasons with the club. He set the franchise goalie record with 240 wins, and twice helped the team reach the Stanley Cup Finals (in 1987 and 1997)! His passionate approach and gutsy playing style inspired fans. His goals were two of many exciting and memorable moments Hextall provided Flyers fans!

The Legion of Doom Thrills Fans; Eric Lindros Tears Through the East in 1997

AFTER LOSING IN THE 1989 CONFERENCE FINALS, the Flyers regressed, missing the playoffs the next three years. In 1992, trying to turn things around, they made a massive trade, acquiring star prospect Eric Lindros from Quebec for Ron Hextall, Peter Forsberg, four other players, two first round draft picks, and $15 million! The Flyers built their team around the huge talent of Lindros, but still missed the playoffs his first two years.

In 1995 things started off looking the same as the Flyers began the season 3–7–1, but everything changed when GM Bobby Clarke made a shocking trade, sending star Mark Recchi (who still holds the franchise record for most points in a season) to Montreal for Éric Desjardins, John LeClair, and Gilbert Dionne. Right away the line of Lindros, LeClair, and Mikael Renberg set the NHL on fire with their combination of talents. The Flyers immediately improved, and soon the line had a nickname: "the Legion of Doom." With the three dominating, plus with big contributions from Desjardins, Rod Brind'Amour, Chris Therien, and Hextall (who had been reacquired in the off-season), the club got hot, going 25–9–3 in their final 37 games to win the division and advance to the playoffs for the first time since '89! Lindros was particularly spectacular. Big, fast, strong, and incredibly skilled, No. 88 was like a freight train on ice! One of Philly's best players ever, "The

Big E" won the NHL MVP Award during the NHL's lockout-shortened season with 29 goals and 41 assists in just 46 games!

In '95–96 the Legion continued to excel, combining for 121 goals and 134 assists as the Flyers had the best record in their conference! In '96–97 they had another big year with 104 goals and 131 assists! In the first three rounds of the '97 playoffs, Lindros was spectacular with 11 goals and 12 assists! This included perhaps his biggest goal ever, a thriller with just 6.8 seconds left versus the Rangers as the Flyers took

Captain Eric Lindros and John LeClair formed one of the great duos in Philly sports history. (Chris Gardner/AP Images)

a 3–1 series lead in the conference finals! The next game the Flyers defeated Wayne Gretzky, Mark Messier, and the Rangers to advance to the Stanley Cup Finals!

Unfortunately, the Flyers lost the '97 Cup to Detroit, and after that Renberg was traded. Although the Flyers got him back in '98, he often played on a different line. Still, Lindros and LeClair continued playing great. In his career with the Flyers, the Big E tallied 290 goals and 369 assists! LeClair, who helped the Flyers reach the playoffs 10 straight seasons, scored 333 goals with 310 assists with the Orange and Black! Lindros was inducted into the Hockey Hall of Fame in 2016! The Lindros and LeClair era was one of the most exciting in Flyers history, and the Legion of Doom remains one of Philly's best combinations of players ever!

Keith Primeau Scores in the Fifth Overtime

IN THE 2000 PLAYOFFS THE FLYERS PLAYED in one of the NHL's most epic games ever, thrilling fans with one of the best endings to a game in Philly sports history. It all started on May 4, 2000, but the game went soooo long it did not end until May 5. That's because it went into overtime, and on this night and into the morning it took a very, very, very long time for either team to score in OT.

Entering the game the Flyers badly needed to win because they trailed the sensational Jaromir Jagr and the Pittsburgh Penguins 2–1 in this Eastern Conference Semifinal series. It all started out very normal. Pittsburgh scored quick in the first period. The Flyers tied it up with a goal by John LeClair early in the third period. But neither team scored after that in regulation, so the game headed into overtime tied 1–1. Whichever team scored next would win.

In the first overtime (a 20-minute period) the energy of the players was pretty good, but neither team scored. In the second overtime the players' energy started to decrease a bit, and again neither team scored. In the third OT it was obvious that both teams were very tired. Still, neither team scored. Flyers goaltender Brian Boucher and Pittsburgh goalie Ron Tugnutt were just too good. In the fourth overtime again neither team scored. Flyers fans watching at home on TV were tired themselves as they would normally be in bed. It was now past 2:00 AM!

During the fifth overtime at 2:35 AM in the game's eighth period, Flyers forward Keith Primeau skated down the right-hand side of the ice carrying the puck, and with a nifty move created enough space to suddenly shoot a quick shot. Tugnutt was unable to stop the puck, which went into the net, finally giving the Flyers the win 12 minutes and one second into the fifth overtime! The Flyers bench erupted in celebration, pouring onto the ice to congratulate Primeau! They also congratulated Boucher, who had stopped a ridiculous 57 of 58 shots!

The Orange and Black rode the momentum from this epic victory, winning their next two games to advance to the Eastern Conference Finals. Boucher's big night and Primeau's thrilling goal provided an instant classic for Philadelphia sports fans who will always remember this remarkable playoff win in the fifth overtime!

Down 3–0 / 3–0 Flyers Complete an Amazing Comeback ... and Reach the Finals

AFTER LOSING IN THE 1997 FINALS, the Flyers did not get back there for a while. In 2000 they blew a 3–1 series lead, losing a heartbreaking Game 7 one win away from advancing to the Cup. This game was particularly awful, as star Eric Lindros suffered a brutal concussion. He never played for the Flyers again. In 2004 Jeremy Roenick scored a tremendous series-clinching goal in Toronto, and captain Keith Primeau played magnificent playoff hockey for three rounds, but again the Flyers lost a Game 7 so close to getting to the Finals.

By 2010 it had been 13 years since the club was in the Finals. But new coach Peter Laviolette, hired by GM Paul Holmgren 25 games into the season, pushed the squad after an uneven start, and they improved. On the last day of the regular season the Flyers made the playoffs with a tremendous shootout win over the Rangers, as goalie Brian Boucher made the final save to secure a spot in the postseason! In Round 1 they beat the Devils. But in Round 2 versus Boston the Flyers ran into big trouble as they lost the first three games. Only two NHL teams had ever come back to win a series after trailing 3–0. But with Mike Richards, Chris Pronger, Kimmo Timonen, Danny Briére, Jeff Carter, Simon Gagné, Scott Hartnell, and young Claude Giroux (who would go on to become a star), the Flyers still had a shot … a very long shot.

In Game 4 the Flyers survived with a 5–4 win as Gagné scored in OT! In Game 5 they dominated in a 4–0 road win, but Boucher got hurt. He was replaced by longtime minor league goalie Michael Leighton. In Game 6, in his first playoff start, Leighton played terrific as the Flyers won 2–1, forcing a Game 7 in Boston! Game 7 started horribly as the Bruins scored the game's first three goals. It seemed very unlikely the Flyers would come back from this hole. Laviolette called a timeout to urge his team to play better. After the timeout they did just that. James van Riemsdyk scored late in the first period, and then Hartnell scored in the second making it 3–2! Halfway through the second period Briére scored, tying the game up 3–3! Then with seven minutes left in the third period, Gagné scored a thrilling goal, giving the Flyers a 4–3 lead! Incredibly, the Flyers now had the edge! Leighton then kept Boston from scoring the rest of the way, as the Orange and Black completed the stunning and historic comeback! Fans celebrated back home as the Flyers won after trailing 3–0 in the series and after trailing 3–0 in Game 7!

The Flyers awesome postseason was not done yet, as they next faced Montreal in the conference finals. Leighton, seemingly out of nowhere, was playing remarkable, posting three shutouts versus the Canadiens!

Simon Gagne celebrates his third period go-ahead goal in Game 7 of the 2010 Eastern Conference Semifinal series versus Boston. (Michael Dwyer/AP Images)

The highlight of the series was provided by Richards, the Flyers captain, who in Game 5 delivered a thunderous hit and scored a goal in what came to be known as "the Shift!" With a Game 5 win, the Flyers were headed to the Stanley Cup Finals!

In the Cup Finals, despite the outstanding play of Pronger, who would eventually make the Hockey Hall of Fame, the Flyers fell to Chicago in a very hard-fought series, four games to two. Still, fans were very proud and grateful for this excellent and unexpected playoff run!

SIXERS

Trading for Wilt Chamberlain

WILT CHAMBERLAIN IS ONE OF THE GREATEST PLAYERS to ever play sports. Wilt's athletic dominance was obvious to anyone who saw him on the playgrounds in Philly long before he even played in the NBA. Growing up in West Philadelphia, Wilt was six feet tall at the age of 10! He was 6'11" as he entered Overbrook High School!

After Wilt's years in college at the University of Kansas (and one year playing with the Harlem Globetrotters), Philly sports fans were excited when the Philadelphia Warriors selected him with what was called a territorial pick in the 1959 NBA Draft. Wilt immediately tore apart the league. In his rookie season he averaged 37.6 points per game! In his third season he averaged an unbelievable 50.4 points! He even scored 100 points in a single game! Wilt was also a tremendous rebounder. One season he averaged 27.2 rebounds! One game he set an NBA record by grabbing 55 of them!

But in 1962, following his third season in the NBA, the Warriors left Philly, moving to San Francisco to become the San Francisco Warriors. It was a rough blow for Philadelphia sports fans because they were losing their pro basketball team (the Sixers did not yet exist in 1962), and losing Wilt, the hometown star. He continued to excel in San Francisco for 2½ seasons, but in 1965 the team around Wilt wasn't very good, and their owner wanted to make a change by trading him.

By this time Philadelphia had a new pro hoops team because the Syracuse Nationals had moved to Philly in 1963, creating the Philadelphia 76ers. The Sixers decided to try to get Wilt back to Philly by offering the Warriors $150,000 plus three players in a trade. Fortunately, the Warriors owner accepted the deal! Wilt was coming back to Philly to play for the Sixers! He immediately made the team a much better squad. Over the next few seasons he put together some of the most extraordinary performances in NBA history. In one game he recorded a "Triple-Double-Double" scoring 22 points with 25 rebounds and 21 assists! He even led the league one year in assists despite being a center! Wilt won three-straight MVP awards with the Sixers! But, despite Wilt's dominance, after his first seven seasons in the league he still had not won an NBA title. The player many considered the best ever was not a champion. That was about to change as the 1966–67 Sixers got ready to rule the NBA.

Sixers Dominate on Their Way to the 1967 Championship

ENTERING THE 1966–67 SEASON, fans in Philly and all around America wondered if the great Wilt Chamberlain would ever win a title. No one knew for sure if he would, but one thing was clear: to win it all the 76ers would have to get past their rival, the Boston Celtics. In 1965 the Celtics beat Wilt and the Sixers 110–109 in Game 7 of the Eastern Finals as John Havlicek stole an inbounds pass in the final seconds to seal the win for Boston. In 1966 the Celtics again defeated the Sixers in the Eastern Finals. The Sixers were very good; the Celtics were simply better.

But in the '66–67 season all that changed as the Sixers, led by GM Jack Ramsay and head coach Alex Hannum, rolled through the NBA. The team started out 7–0. In early January they were 37–3! The Sixers were an absolute force, averaging 125 points per game! When the regular season was over the team's record was an awesome 68–13, the best record up until that point in NBA history! Along the way Wilt changed his game on offense, scoring less while passing more to his talented teammates. Wilt's stats were still exceptional as he averaged 24.1 points, 24.2 rebounds, and 7.8 assists per game! Other stars like future Hall of Famers Hal Greer, Chet Walker, and Billy Cunningham also played a big part in the team's success, as did contributors Luke Jackson and Wali Jones.

But none of the Sixers regular season success would mean much if the squad did not win it all in the playoffs. In the 1967 postseason Wilt had no intention of letting his team blow this great chance at a championship. In the first round the Sixers beat Oscar Robertson and the Cincinnati Royals 3–1. In the second round the Sixers finally defeated Bill Russell and the eight-time defending champion Boston Celtics 4–1! It was sweet revenge for the Sixers and for all Philadelphia sports fans! In the NBA Finals the 76ers faced Wilt's old team, the San

Wilt Chamberlain (No. 13) is the center of attention as the Sixers celebrate beating the Boston Celtics in the playoffs. Two weeks later the Sixers won their first championship. (AP Images)

Francisco Warriors. The Sixers won three of the first five games to take a 3–2 series lead! On **April 24, 1967,** in Game 6, Wilt scored 24 points and grabbed 23 rebounds, and Wali Jones scored 27 points as the Sixers won 125–122 to win the NBA title! Wilt was finally a champion! The Sixers were the very best in basketball!

To this day there are some historians and basketball fans who still believe that the '66–67 Sixers are the best team in NBA history!

Julius Erving Comes to Philly; Team Goes Straight to the Finals

IN THE YEARS AFTER WINNING THE 1967 NBA TITLE, things fell apart for the Sixers. In '68 they traded Wilt Chamberlain to the Los Angeles Lakers. It was terrible news for 76ers fans, but only one of many factors that led to the decline of the team. Chet Walker was also traded. Hal Greer aged and retired. And Billy Cunningham left the Sixers for two years to play in the ABA, a different basketball league. The team became so bad that the 1972–73 Sixers actually finished with nine wins and 73 losses for the worst record in NBA history.

Some help was on the way though, as the Sixers drafted Doug Collins with the No. 1 overall pick in the 1973 Draft. They also acquired talented players George McGinnis, Lloyd Free, and Darryl Dawkins in '75. Despite improving, the 76ers still needed a franchise player. When Julius Erving became available in '76, Sixers management knew he could be the key piece for the team's future.

Erving had already established himself as a big star in the ABA. He went by the nickname "Dr. J," and in five seasons playing in the ABA for the Virginia Squires and the New York Nets he won three MVP awards and two championships. He amazed fans across the country with his incredible dunks! He could jump so far and hang so long in the air while

Dr. J had an amazing ability to glide to the basket or throw down a massive dunk in ways that fans had never seen before he played. (Bettmann/Getty Images)

twisting his body with grace and power to dunk the ball or lay it in! Nobody had ever seen anyone else play basketball like Dr J!

Prior to the '76–77 season, four teams from the ABA, including the Nets, joined the NBA. At that time, Dr. J and the Nets were in a salary dispute, so the Nets decided to trade him. The Sixers offered $3 million to get "Doc," and the Nets agreed to the deal! The great Dr. J would play for the 76ers!

In his first season in Philly, Dr. J was fantastic as he entertained fans at the Spectrum with his unique brand of offensive basketball. He helped the squad quickly become one of the best teams in the league as they went 50–32 in the regular season. The Sixers then advanced through their conference in the playoffs, making it all the way to the NBA Finals! They lost in six games to Portland in a very disappointing series, but despite this everyone knew Doc was a truly special player. With Dr. J as the team's new star, fans were excited for the Sixers future!

Sixers Get to the 1980 Finals During an Incredible Year in Philly Sports

FOLLOWING THEIR LOSS IN THE 1977 NBA FINALS, the Sixers made another strong push in '78, but lost in the Eastern Conference Finals. After the season the team traded scorer George McGinnis for Bobby Jones, a defensive wizard who also had offensive capabilities. Jones, who would turn into a huge fan favorite, went on to complement Julius Erving's game for the next eight years. However, in '79 the Sixers took a step backward as they were ousted in the second round of the playoffs.

The following year the Sixers rebounded, and in doing so set off one of the most extraordinary achievements for a city in sports history. Dr. J was at or near the top of his athletic greatness averaging an awesome 26.9 points, 7.4 rebounds, 4.6 assists, 2.2 steals, and 1.8 blocks per game!

Others contributed, such as Jones, Darryl Dawkins, Caldwell Jones, Doug Collins, Maurice Cheeks, Lionel Hollins, Steve Mix, and Henry Bibby. The Sixers handled the Eastern Conference in the playoffs in route to the NBA Finals for the second time in four seasons!

Unfortunately, the Sixers lost the Finals to the Lakers in six games. LA got a huge lift from rookie Magic Johnson, who played great in Game 6 while center Kareem Abdul-Jabbar sat out with an injury. It was a rough loss for Philly sports fans, even though they knew the Sixers were primed for more success in future years.

What fans did not know at that time was just how unbelievable 1980 would be in Philly sports. That is because in '80 Philadelphia accomplished the phenomenal feat of having all four of its teams advance to their sport's title round in the same year! That is, if you count the 1980 Eagles, who played most of their season in '80, but reached the Super Bowl in early 1981. For a few months Philly was the center of the sports world! The Sixers played in the NBA Finals starting on May 4, 1980! The Flyers played in the Stanley Cup Finals starting on May 13, 1980! The Phillies played in the World Series starting on October 14, 1980! And the Eagles played in the Super Bowl on January 25, 1981! This remains the only time one town had four of its teams play in the championship round in such a short span of time! It will likely never happen again, but that does not have to stop you from dreaming that it might. Sure, it was a bummer that only the Phils won it all that year, but fans who were alive in 1980 will always remember this sensational year in sports!

A Game 7 Win in Boston

THE 76ERS AND BOSTON CELTICS RIVALRY has been one of the very best and most bitter rivalries in the history of sports. Matchups between players and battles between the teams have been legendary. Wilt

Chamberlain versus the great Bill Russell. Dr. J against Celtics star Larry Bird. It was compelling as the Sixers and Celtics often pushed each other to the limit with fierce games in front of intense fans.

So it was in the early 1980s as the 76ers and Celtics competed in some of the hardest-fought playoff series in NBA history. The '81 Eastern Conference Finals was brutal for any Sixers fan. Leading 3–1 in the series, with just one more win needed to reach the Finals, the 76ers lost three straight games to lose the series 4–3.

In '82 the Sixers again held a 3–1 series lead over Boston in the conference finals. Philly fans were hoping the Sixers would quickly close out the series, but they lost the next two forcing a Game 7 in the famed Boston Garden. Few people around the country gave the 76ers much of a chance to win Game 7 in Boston. The '82 Celtics were led by Bird, one of the most exceptional players in league history, but they also had other stars like Kevin McHale and Robert Parish. The Sixers were still led by Dr. J, and while he played fantastic in Game 7, scoring 29 points, it was one of the 76ers youngest players that shined brightest in the deciding game. His name: Andrew Toney. His nickname: "The Boston Strangler." Toney's Game 7 dominance in Boston is one of the most spectacular big-game performances under pressure ever by a Philly athlete. With so much on the line, Toney, a second-year guard, delivered all game long. He scored going to the hole. He had a great mid-range game. He hit jumpers from the outside. Boston couldn't stop him! In the fourth quarter as the Sixers pulled away, coach Billy Cunningham famously raised his fist with determination and excitement! Toney finished with 34 points as the Sixers won Game 7 120–106! They had not blown the series like they did in 1981. The 76ers had defeated the Celtics in Boston, and as Celtics fans incredibly chanted "Beat LA," the Sixers were headed to the 1982 NBA Finals!

The Sixers lost the '82 Finals in six games, but they were still primed for a fantastic future, and fans knew one move could put them over the top the following year.

'83 Sixers Romp Through the NBA for the Title

DESPITE REACHING THE NBA FINALS with Julius Erving in 1977, 1980, and 1982, the Sixers just could not get over the hump in those years to win the title. In '77 they lost to Portland 4–2 after leading the series 2–0. After that series the Sixers came up with a slogan for fans, saying "We Owe You One." In '80 the Sixers lost to the Lakers as rookie Magic Johnson led the way for LA in Game 6. And in '82 the Sixers again lost to Magic, Kareem Abdul-Jabbar, and the Lakers in six games. It seemed that perhaps the Sixers would not win a championship with Dr. J.

While guards Mo Cheeks and Andrew Toney were excellent young players, and forward Bobby Jones was outstanding as well, the legendary Dr. J was 32 years old after the '82 season, which meant he probably would not have too many great years left in his career. The Sixers front office, led by owner Harold Katz and GM Pat Williams, wanted to do something different to push the team over the top to win the title, and they had just the right guy in mind to try to get: Moses Malone.

In the late 1970s and early '80s Houston Rockets center Moses Malone was one of the strongest forces in basketball, twice winning the league's MVP award. He also helped Houston reach the NBA Finals in 1981. When he became available in the summer of '82 the Sixers swooped in and traded for him! Everybody in Philadelphia hoped Moses would lead the 76ers to the title in '83.

When the '82–83 season started it was obvious right away that with Moses in the middle the Sixers were a spectacular team. They won their first six games. By late November they were 13–2. By mid-January they were an amazing 34–5! Coach Billy Cunningham had the Sixers playing tremendous team basketball. With role players Marc Iavaroni, Clint Richardson, and Clemon Johnson contributing, the Sixers were not just strong on offense; they played elite defensive basketball too.

In the 1983 NBA All-Star Game the Sixers showcased something special and rare: four players from the same team in the All-Star Game! Cheeks, Toney, Dr. J, and Moses all played together in the game with the top players in the world!

After the All-Star break the 76ers domination of the league continued. When the regular season ended, the Sixers finished with an awesome 65–17 record, which up until that point was the fourth-best mark in an 82-game season in league history! But the Sixers knew based on their playoff defeats in the past that fans would be very disappointed if they did not win the title in '83. The Sixers were a confident group, and nothing showed that more than Moses' prediction before the postseason when he said the 76ers would go "Fo-Fo-Fo" in the playoffs. This meant that Moses thought the Sixers would win all three of their playoff series four games to none.

In the playoffs the Sixers swept the New York Knicks 4–0 in the first round. Then they won the first three games versus the Milwaukee Bucks in the Eastern Conference Finals before losing Game 4 in Milwaukee. The Sixers bounced back with a Game 5 victory, winning the series 4–1 to advance to the NBA Finals! For the third time in four years they would face Magic, Kareem, and the Lakers for the title. But this year the 76ers had Moses!

The Sixers won Game 1 and Game 2 in Philly, and then won Game 3 in LA to take a 3–0 series lead! Moses was crushing Kareem with physical play in the paint. For the series Moses averaged 25.8 points and 18 rebounds per game, while Kareem averaged 23.5 points but only 7.5 rebounds. Philly fans were thinking this would finally be the Sixers year. On **May 31, 1983,** the Sixers and Lakers battled in Game 4 as LA put up a fight, leading Philly by 11 points entering the fourth quarter. But the Sixers rallied, cutting into the lead, and then Dr. J took over. Doc scored seven straight Sixers points on a steal and dunk with two minutes to go, a fast-break three-point play on a layup while getting fouled with 59 seconds left, and then hit a key jump shot giving the 76ers a three-point lead with 24 seconds remaining! It was fitting given Doc's huge impact for so many years that he starred in this moment!

Then, after a defensive stop, Moses hammered in a huge dunk as the Sixers bench began to celebrate! After one more defensive stop, Cheeks romped down the floor, slamming the ball at the buzzer as the Sixers won the championship with a 115–108 win! The Sixers had done it! Dr. J finally had his title in the NBA with the 76ers! Moses, with an awesome 24 points and 23 rebounds in Game 4, had led the 76ers to the championship, and along the way captured both the regular season MVP Award and the NBA Finals MVP Award! It wasn't "Fo-Fo-Fo." It was "Fo-Five-Fo!" The '83 76ers had completed their mission, and in doing so established themselves as perhaps the best team in Philadelphia sports history!

Dr. J (left) and Moses Malone (right) hold the championship trophy after the Sixers swept the Lakers to win the 1983 NBA title. (AP Images)

A Special Retirement Season for Dr. J

IN 1986 JULIUS ERVING ANNOUNCED that the upcoming season would be his last as a player. Dr. J was a beloved figure not just in Philly but all around the country. He had thrilled fans for years with unique moves on the court such as his around-the-backboard layup against the Lakers in 1980 and his "Rock The Baby" windmill dunk over Michael Cooper in 1983! American sports fans embraced Doc because of his greatness as a player, but also because they liked him as a person and appreciated how he helped improve the NBA. That is why in 1986 all the NBA teams decided to do something special; they would honor Dr. J with a ceremony in their home arena prior to the 76ers final game against them in the 1986–87 season so fans from each NBA town could thank Doc for his contributions to the game. Never before had such an incredible gesture been extended to one athlete!

All season, in every NBA city, Dr. J was honored before games. Even Boston and LA, the 76ers biggest rivals, honored Doc. In his final regular season home game, the Sixers put together the grandest ceremony of all, as Philly fans showed Doc the love. After the pregame ceremony, Dr. J scored 38 points to reach the 30,000-point club, joining Kareem Abdul-Jabbar and Wilt Chamberlain at that time as the only three players to score 30,000 points in a pro career (ABA & NBA combined)!

In the playoffs the Sixers lost to the Bucks, dropping Game 5 in Milwaukee. As Dr. J was taken out of the game ending his career, he received a massive standing ovation from Bucks fans! CBS announcer Dick Stockton said, "All of the lasting words fit this man: ambassador, statesman, he transcended sports. Genuine athletic hero. Never a bad word about him. Where does he rank and what kind of company? I don't know. Maybe Jesse Owens, Jackie Robinson, Joe DiMaggio. People like that!" When the game ended, Doc held up a basketball, saluting the crowd as the *Rocky* theme song played and Bucks fans gave him one final ovation!

Throughout his career Dr. J performed with class, athletic flair, and excellence. He was one of sport's most spectacular entertainers. In the ABA Doc was a five-time All-Star, three-time MVP, and two-time champion. In the NBA he was an 11-time All-Star, an MVP, and a champion with the '83 Sixers! He will always be remembered as one of the most beloved players in Philadelphia and in American sports history!

The Great Charles Barkley

IN 1984 THE 76ERS SELECTED CHARLES BARKLEY from Auburn with the fifth pick in the NBA Draft. It was a risky choice because Barkley was a 6'4" forward who at times weighed close to 300 pounds. He had been cut from the '84 US Olympic team. Fans wondered if Barkley could control his weight to become a good NBA player.

In his early years Barkley teamed with the stars from the Sixers '83 title squad, but age and injuries made them less effective. The 76ers also made horrible moves, trading Moses Malone and the No. 1 overall pick in the '86 Draft. All of this hurt the Sixers chances for team success with Barkley. It was not his fault. Nevertheless, Barkley played remarkable basketball his entire time in Philly. He took off in year two, averaging 20 points. He played with tremendous competitive fire and had exceptional athletic talents, such as his awesome leaping ability and immense strength. In his third year "the Round Mound of Rebound" led the NBA with 14.6 rebounds per game! In his fourth season he averaged 28.3 points! Barkley became an absolute force! He could out-rebound much taller players, score in the post with incredible quickness and strength, and go end-to-end, ripping down defensive rebounds before finishing with powerful jams on the other end! Fans had never seen a player quite like Barkley. Plus, "Sir Charles" entertained fans with his huge, outrageous personality. He would say and do things other players would not.

The 1989–90 season was the highlight of his eight years in Philly. Joining forces with Rick Mahorn to form "Thump & Bump," while also playing alongside Johnny Dawkins, Hersey Hawkins, and Mike Gminski, Barkley was spectacular, averaging 25.2 points, 11.5 rebounds, 3.9 assists, and 1.9 steals while shooting 60 percent from the field!

Charles Barkley brought an amazing combination of power, quickness, and skill to the 76ers during his Hall of Fame career. (Bob Galbraith/AP Images)

Jimmy Lynam's squad won their division, and Barkley finished second for MVP.

Sadly, the 76ers made the huge mistake of trading Barkley in '92. He went on to better team success with the Suns and Rockets, and also won Olympic gold in '92 (on the Dream Team) and in '96. He was named one of the NBA's 50 Greatest Players during the league's 50th anniversary season in '97. Barkley made fans proud as he wore a 76ers jacket during the ceremony even though he was a member of the Rockets at the time! Sir Charles, who appreciated what Philadelphia and the Sixers meant to him, will always be one of Philly's greatest and most entertaining players!

Winning the 1996 Draft Lottery; Selecting Allen Iverson No. 1 Overall

AFTER TRADING CHARLES BARKLEY IN 1992, the Sixers completely fell apart. They became a truly terrible team, and their record each year showed it. The 76ers were 26–56 in '92–'93, 25–57 in '93–94, 24–58 in '94–95, and 18–64 in '95–96. They badly needed better players. As the 1996 NBA Draft Lottery approached, fans realized Georgetown's very talented guard Allen Iverson would likely be the No. 1 pick in the draft. If the Sixers could get the top pick, they would be able to select Iverson and bring excitement back to fans. The Sixers sent minority owner and team president Pat Croce to represent them at the lottery. Croce brought two good luck charms along: a Waterford Crystal from Ireland and a medal from his late father. The Sixers would need luck; they had a 33.73 percent chance to land the No. 1 pick in the draft. As the lottery unfolded everyone waited for the results, and when they were revealed, the 76ers had won the draft lottery! Croce stood up and

Allen Iverson holds up a Sixers jersey after being selected with the No. 1 overall pick in the 1996 NBA Draft. (Stan Honda/Getty Images)

high-fived people around him! Fans in Philly celebrated! Iverson would be a Sixer!

In his first year "The Answer" immediately thrilled fans with his play. His abilities were phenomenal. He was likely the quickest player in NBA history, physically tough, and very competitive. As one of the league's smallest players, there had never been anyone quite like Iverson. He entertained fans with his scoring, brought hope back to the Sixers, and won the Rookie of the Year Award in 1997!

The Sixers were far from a finished product though, so Croce made a major move after "AI's" first year by hiring Larry Brown to be the Sixers new coach. Brown and Iverson often battled, but they both helped the 76ers improve a lot. Brown also added role players to fit around Iverson. Team success would follow, and individual success for AI as well. In 11 seasons with the Sixers he averaged 27.6 points, 3.9 rebounds, 6.1 assists, and 2.3 steals per game! He was a seven-time All-Star with the Sixers, while winning four league scoring titles and the 2001 NBA MVP Award! He forged a Hall of Fame career! Perhaps more than anything, Iverson is viewed as an all-time Philly sports fan-favorite. His small size, emotional nature, willingness to be vulnerable, skill, plus his all-out effort on the court driven by a deep desire to win captured the hearts of Philly sports fans! This was never truer than in 2001 when Iverson and the Sixers went on a magical run.

2001 Sixers Prove AI, Larry Brown, and Heart Can Take You Far

THE 2001 SIXERS ARE ONE OF THE MOST BELOVED TEAMS ever in Philadelphia. They did not win the NBA title, but their passionate play and determination inspired fans during a phenomenal season. This team had skill and one elite player in Allen Iverson, but it was their heart and will to battle and win that made them so special.

The '01 Sixers were the result of great vision and effort over many years by minority owner and team president Pat Croce, coach Larry Brown, and GM Billy King, who had all worked tirelessly to improve the squad. After reaching the second round of the playoffs in '99 and '00, the 76ers entered AI's fifth season hoping to go further. Right away they were on fire, beginning the season 10–0! In addition to Iverson, the Sixers also relied on role players that Brown and King had acquired, such as Eric Snow, George Lynch, Tyrone Hill, Theo Ratliff, Aaron McKie, and Toni Kukoč. They played great defense, AI handled the offensive load, and the team found ways to win close games in the fourth quarter. Iverson, with his remarkable speed, gutsy play, and toughness, was dominating on his way to the best season of his career. By the All-Star break they were 36–14. In the All-Star Game Iverson starred, winning the MVP award! Then he delighted fans during an interview as he sought out Brown by saying, "Where my coach? Where my coach? Coach Brown!" He wanted to share the moment with his coach. Philly was in love with the '01 Sixers!

But Ratliff got hurt, which meant he might miss the rest of his year, so Brown traded him, Kukoč, and two others for All-Star center Dikembe Mutombo. The 76ers stumbled at first with Dikembe in the lineup, but then hit their stride, finishing the regular season 56–26 for the best record in their conference! Awards came rolling in. Iverson was named league MVP! Brown, with one of the most masterful Philly coaching jobs ever, received the Coach of the Year Award! Mutombo earned the Defensive Player of the Year Award! And McKie was named the NBA's Sixth Man of the Year! It was incredible to see one team win four prominent league awards!

In the first round of the playoffs the Sixers faced the star and squad that knocked them out of the postseason the previous two years: Reggie Miller and the Pacers. Things felt shaky when Indiana won Game 1 in Philly, but the Sixers shook it off to win three straight to take the series 3–1! Fans throughout the Philly area caught 76ers playoff fever,

Allen Iverson steps over Tyronn Lue after making a huge shot during overtime in Game 1 of the 2001 NBA Finals. (Otto Greule Jr./Getty Images)

and began to proudly display Sixers flags out the window of their cars! The Sixers were the talk of the town. They even appeared on the front page of the *Philadelphia Daily News* for over a month straight during the playoffs!

Next up in the second round was Vince Carter and the Toronto Raptors. The Sixers again lost Game 1, but they again bounced back in Game 2 as AI was presented with his regular season MVP Award that night. After giving a great pregame speech to the crowd, Iverson scored 54 points, the first of two 50-plus-point games for him in the series! Back and forth it went in this tough series as AI and Carter battled. Finally, in Game 7, with Toronto down one point, Carter missed a shot at the buzzer as the Sixers advanced to the conference finals behind Iverson's 21 points and 16 assists!

In the conference finals the Sixers faced Ray Allen and the Bucks. The Sixers had a lot of injuries. AI couldn't play in Game 3, which the Sixers lost to fall into a 2–1 hole. But he played in Game 4 as the 76ers evened the series 2–2! Eventually the series was pushed to the limit. In Game 7, in front of a packed crowd at the First Union Center, Iverson's 44 points, six rebounds, and seven assists, in addition to Mutombo's 23 points, 19 rebounds, and seven blocks led the Sixers to a thrilling victory! Philly partied hard as the 76ers were headed to the Finals for the first time in 18 years!

In the Finals the 76ers squared off with Shaquille O'Neal, Kobe Bryant, and the defending champion Los Angeles Lakers, who came in with a 19-game winning streak. Many people in America thought the Sixers had no shot to win. In Game 1 Iverson amazed the nation, leading the Sixers to victory by scoring 48 points! In overtime the most memorable moment of AI's career occurred when he hit a key jumper and then stepped over Tyron Lue of the Lakers! It was yet another thrill!

Unfortunately, the Sixers numerous injuries and the Lakers greatness caught up to the 76ers. They were giving it every ounce of effort they had, but as the series wore on it became obvious that Shaq and Kobe's Lakers were just too good. The Sixers dream of a championship died in Game 5 as LA won the series 4–1. Nevertheless, anybody who witnessed the

2001 Sixers will never forget the spirit they played with or the awesome journey they took Philly sports fans on. Iverson and his squad proved that heart, guts, and determination can take a team very far. In the process the 2001 Sixers became one of Philly's favorite teams ever!

The Immensely Talented Joel Embiid

FOLLOWING THE 76ERS RUN TO THE FINALS IN 2001, they got back to the playoffs only three more times with Allen Iverson. The Sixers eventually traded AI in 2006. In time they built around Andre Iguodala, Elton Brand, Jrue Holiday, Lou Williams, and Thaddeus Young, but even though this group had some playoff success in 2012, they were not a title contender. In 2013 new GM Sam Hinkie came up with a controversial plan to try to help the Sixers become elite. While he never admitted it publicly, everyone knew Hinkie wanted the 76ers to lose games so they would have better odds to win the NBA Draft Lottery in order to hopefully get better players. As a result, the Sixers began their "tanking" years. Many fans loved the approach. Many fans hated the approach. Over time this strategy came to be known as "The Process." From 2013 to '17 the Sixers acquired seven players drafted in the lottery. Of these, six had no positive impact on the team long-term, but one of them, Joel Embiid, a 7'2" center from Cameroon, Africa, and the University of Kansas became a star!

Embiid missed his first two pro seasons due to an injury. In the first year he played, Embiid was great, but got hurt after only 31 games. However, in his fourth year the Sixers finally became a contender again, reaching the playoffs in 2018. In the years that followed as the Sixers made the postseason seven straight times, Embiid became one of the NBA's top players. His immense size coupled with unique athleticism, quality shooting, and elite defense made him a force! Twice he was runner-up for MVP, and then in 2023 he won the MVP Award, only the

Joel Embiid lifts his MVP trophy during a ceremony honoring him in 2023. (Tim Nwachukwu/Getty Images)

fifth Sixers player to do so! The next year Embiid scored 70 points in a game, and remarkably became the first player since Wilt Chamberlain to average more than a point per minute played for an entire season! In his first nine years playing, Embiid averaged an awesome 27.7 points, 11 rebounds, 3.7 assists, and 1.6 blocks per game while shooting 50.1 percent from the field and 82.8 percent from the line! He also won gold in the 2024 Summer Olympics!

Frustratingly, Embiid's career has been hurt by injuries, often in the playoffs. The Sixers with Embiid have yet to live up to their full potential. They have surrounded Embiid with the wrong teammates, and he has let them down at times. Still, with his incredible talent, Embiid is one of the most skilled NBA big men ever!

EAGLES

Steve Van Buren Leads the 1948 and 1949 Eagles to the Championship

UNTIL THE EAGLES WON IT ALL IN THE 2017 SEASON, the Birds had never won the Super Bowl, but that does not mean they had never won a championship. The Super Bowl did not exist until the late 1960s. Prior to that, the Eagles, who began play in 1933 when they were founded by Bert Bell and Lud Wray, won the NFL title game three times, including in back-to-back seasons in 1948 and '49. Those years the team's main star was bruising running back Steve Van Buren. He led the NFL in rushing four times. The Birds QB, Tommy Thompson, was legally blind in one eye! Other standouts included future Hall of Famers Alex Wojciechowicz and Pete Pihos, in addition to Bucko Kilroy and Al Wistert. The head coach was Earle "Greasy" Neale.

In 1948, after a loss and tie to start the year, the Eagles got hot, winning nine of 10 to finish 9–2–1. Back then the postseason format was very different than today. The Birds advanced right to the NFL Championship Game, where they were set to face the Cardinals in Philly. However, the Cards were not the only foe on **December 19, 1948**. There was a huge snowstorm! Van Buren, thinking the game would be postponed, delayed leaving his home. When he finally left, he could not get his car out of the driveway! So he took a bus, then a trolley, then the subway, and then he walked to Shibe Park! He got there only 30 minutes before the scheduled kickoff! There was so much snow players even had to help remove the tarp covering the field. When the game began the teams struggled on offense. However, Van Buren kept fighting through the snow for 98 tough yards, and in the fourth quarter he scored the game's only TD, helping the Eagles win 7–0 to capture their first championship!

In 1949 the Eagles were even better as they finished the regular season with an awesome 11–1 record! They crushed teams, winning

49–14, 38–7, 38–14, 44–21, 42–0, 34–17, and 24–3! In the title game on **December 18, 1949,** the Eagles faced the Rams in the LA Coliseum. Van Buren, clutch again, was tremendous as he rushed 31 times for 196 yards! The Eagles defense again shut out their opponent in the title game as the Birds won 14–0 to capture their second championship!

The '48 and '49 Eagles are two of Philly's special teams, and Van Buren clearly is one of the Birds best players ever! When he retired, Van Buren was the NFL's career rushing leader! In 1965 he was inducted into the Pro Football Hall of Fame!

Steve Van Buren (No. 15) plows through the snow to plunge into the end zone for the only touchdown in the 1948 NFL Championship Game. (AP Images)

Chuck Bednarik Plays Both Ways as the Eagles Win the Title in 1960

IN 1949 THE EAGLES SELECTED PENN'S CHUCK BEDNARIK with the No. 1 overall pick in the NFL Draft. Over the next 14 years "Concrete Charlie" made eight Pro Bowls and emerged as one of the greatest and toughest players in NFL history. Part of what made Bednarik so exceptional was that sometimes he would play and excel on both offense and defense in the same game! On offense he would play center. On defense he would play linebacker. Bednarik starred in the 1950s, but the Birds had not won a title since 1949. That changed in 1960, as a great Eagles team with Bednarik, QB and league MVP Norm Van Brocklin, WR Tommy McDonald, TE Pete Retzlaff, LB Maxie Baughan, DB Tom Brookshier, and other standouts rolled through the league. In November of '60 Bednarik delivered his most legendary hit, brutally tackling Giants star Frank Gifford! The Birds went 10–2 during the regular season!

On **December 26, 1960,** the Eagles, with Buck Shaw as head coach, faced Vince Lombardi's Green Bay Packers in the NFL Championship Game at Franklin Field in Philly. Bednarik decided he would do everything possible to help the Eagles win, so he played every play on offense and every play on defense. That's right: Bednarik played every offensive and defensive snap for an entire 60-minute NFL game!

The 1960 title game was a back-and-forth contest. Green Bay got the scoring going with two field goals, but the Eagles answered in the second quarter with a TD pass from "The Dutchman" (Van Brocklin) to McDonald as the Birds took a 7–6 lead! After the Eagles kicked a field goal, Green Bay scored a fourth-quarter touchdown to take a 13–10 lead. The Eagles needed to score, and with five minutes left in the game, Birds running back Ted Dean ran five yards for a touchdown, giving the Eagles a 17–13 lead! The Eagles defense now had to stop Green Bay from scoring, but the Packers moved down the field. On the final play of the game Green Bay star Jim Taylor caught a pass, but Bednarik tackled him at the 9-yard line and stayed on top of Taylor long enough for the clock to run out! The game was over! Bednarik had made the key play at the end! The 1960 Eagles were champions!

For his tremendous career, Bednarik was inducted into the Pro Football Hall of Fame in 1967! He remains one of the most extraordinary players and one of the most legendary warriors in Philadelphia and American sports history!

The Meadowlands: A Place Where Miracles Happen

MIRACLES DO NOT HAPPEN OFTEN, but they sure do seem to happen when the Eagles play on the road versus one of their classic rivals: the New York Giants. Four times the Birds have pulled off something shocking—a "Miracle"—late on the road against the Giants to win a game. Each time the Eagles advanced that season to make the playoffs. These games were all very meaningful on the journey to the postseason. They were all miraculous!

Miracle No. 1: November 19, 1978

With under two minutes left in the fourth quarter, the Giants had the ball and led 17–12. All New York needed to do was have their quarterback, Joe Pisarcik, fall to the ground after getting the snap for a few plays to run out the clock (the NFL had not yet put in the rule whereby a QB could simply "take a knee" to run out the clock). On first down Pisarcik purposely fell down, but Eagles linebacker Frank LeMaster smashed into a Giants running back and came crashing in over top of Pisarcik. This annoyed the Giants. On second down they ran a regular rushing play, with fullback Larry Csonka gaining positive yards. Incredibly,

Herman Edwards (No. 46) gets ready to scoop up the football seconds before racing into the end zone to win the game with "the Miracle at the Meadowlands." (G. Paul Burnett/AP Images)

on third down, still irritated with LeMaster and the Eagles, the Giants offensive coordinator (who would be fired the next day) again called a regular running play. Pisarcik took the snap and attempted to hand the ball to Csonka, but Pisarcik bobbled and then fumbled the football! Birds cornerback Herman Edwards scooped up the ball on one hop and ran straight into the end zone for an Eagles TD! The Birds won the game! "The Miracle At The Meadowlands" remains one of the most shocking plays in NFL history! And it was crucial for the Birds to make the postseason in '78 for the first time in 18 years!

Miracle No. 2: November 20, 1988

Exactly one day after the 10-year anniversary of the Miracle At The Meadowlands, the Eagles and Giants were tied 17–17 in overtime. The Birds lined up for a 31-yard field goal that could win the game, but Giants superstar Lawrence Taylor blocked the field-goal attempt.

Fortunately, the ball was quickly retrieved on one bounce by Eagles player Clyde Simmons behind the line of scrimmage. Simmons, who rarely touched the football because he was usually a defensive lineman, started running with the ball, and soon he crossed the goal line for a TD! Many people were confused. Did this count as a touchdown? It did! The Eagles won the game 23–17! This remains the only time in NFL history that the kicking team won a game in overtime by running in a blocked field goal!

Miracle No. 3: October 19, 2003

Entering the 2003 season, expectations were high for the Eagles, but they started the year 2–3, and in their sixth game versus the Giants the Birds were in deep trouble and struggling on offense. They trailed 10–7 with 1:34 to go in the fourth quarter. It looked like the Eagles were shockingly about to be 2–4 on the season. As the Giants got set to punt, second-year Birds player Brian Westbrook waited to return it. The punt bounced at the Eagles 21-yard line, and Westbrook caught it on one hop at the 16-yard line. He immediately made one Giants defender miss, then others, and ran with tremendous speed up the left sideline. At midfield he got by one last Giant, and from there B-West was off to the races! He ran all the way down the field for a touchdown! The Birds won the game, and then went on to win eight more in a row after that! To this day, many Eagles fans still say that with his huge punt return for a touchdown "Brian Westbrook saved the season!"

Miracle No. 4: December 19, 2010

In a key 2010 game the Eagles trailed the Giants 31–10 with eight minutes to go in the fourth quarter. It seemed the Birds had almost no chance to win. But then the Eagles came alive, playing almost perfect the rest of the way. Brent Celek scored a 65-yard TD on a pass from Michael Vick to make it 31–17 with 7:28 left. The Eagles then recovered an onside kick, and Vick quickly scored on a run to make it 31–24 with 5:28 to go! The Eagles defense then stopped the Giants offense, and when the Birds got the ball back, Vick, in the midst of his best season, threw a TD to Jeremy

Maclin to tie the game 31–31 with 1:16 left! After the Eagles defense stopped the Giants offense again, New York was forced to punt with 14 seconds left. Punter Matt Dodge was instructed by his coaches to punt the ball away from Eagles punt returner DeSean Jackson, but Dodge accidentally kicked the ball right toward him. DeSean initially dropped the ball, but then he picked it up, moved backward, and suddenly burst forward through a group of players! He raced all the way down the field in the clear to score, but as he approached the goal line DeSean decided to run across the field near the goal line to make sure time had expired before finally going into the end zone for the TD! DeSean had done it! The Eagles had done it! They pulled off another miracle! In the process, DeSean became the first NFL player to score a touchdown on a punt return on the final play of the fourth quarter to win a game!

DeSean Jackson races down the sideline as Giants coach Tom Coughlin (right) reacts with disgust, knowing the Eagles are about to win the game. (Nick Laham/Getty Images)

Dick Vermeil's 1980 Eagles Beat Dallas in the NFC Championship Game

DESPITE HAVING STANDOUTS IN THE 1960s such as Pete Retzlaff, Maxie Baughan, Sonny Jurgensen, Timmy Brown, and Bob Brown, and Pro Bowlers in the early-to-mid-1970s like Bill Bradley, Harold Jackson, Charle Young, Harold Carmichael, and Bill Bergey, the Birds struggled after winning the title in '60. From '62 to '75 they had only one year with a winning record. In '76, owner Leonard Tose and GM Jim Murray hired Dick Vermeil as their new coach. In time he would become one of the most important figures ever in Philly sports as Vermeil, perhaps more than anyone, elevated the city's passionate connection to the Birds. The Eagles massive impact on our sports culture today in many ways can be traced to Vermeil. But in '76 he was new to town, and had his work cut out for him, especially with the mighty Cowboys in the division. Vermeil constantly told his players they had to track down their rival, Dallas, a squad which had humiliated them for years. Dallas, known as "America's Team," was the target.

In the late 1970s the Eagles made progress, reaching the playoffs in '78 and '79, but Dallas still stood in their way. Vermeil hoped that would change in '80 as QB Ron Jaworski, RB Wilbert Montgomery, WR Carmichael, tackles Stan Walters and Jerry Sisemore, defenders Bergey, Carl Hairston, Claude Humphrey, Frank LeMaster, John Bunting, Herman Edwards, Randy Logan, and others rolled to a 12–4 record! With "Jaws" third for league MVP, the Birds won the NFC East and reached the playoffs for the third year in a row! They began the postseason by beating Minnesota 31–16!

Next up was the showdown Vermeil, Eagles players, and Birds fans wanted: the NFC Championship Game at Veterans Stadium in Philly between the Eagles and the Dallas Cowboys. The Birds got off to a tremendous start as Wilbert rushed for a 42-yard TD on the Eagles

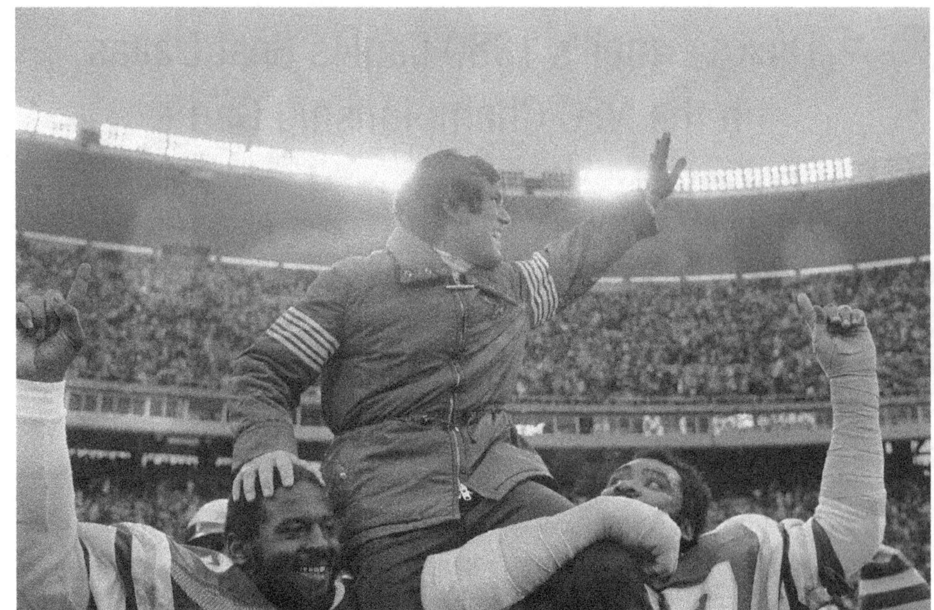

In 1980, Dick Vermeil, Eagles players, and Philadelphia sports fans formed a special bond that has lasted through the decades. (Clem Murray/AP Images)

second play of the game! Dallas tied it up in the second quarter, but after halftime Wilbert continued to punish the Cowboys on his way to 194 rushing yards for the game! The Birds pulled away, thrilling the home crowd as they won 20–7! The Eagles had taken down Dallas, and fans at the Vet celebrated as the Birds were headed to the Super Bowl for the first time in franchise history!

Unfortunately, the Eagles lost Super Bowl XV to the Oakland Raiders, but to this day Wilbert's TD run remains one of the city's most iconic plays, and the Birds' NFC Championship win over Dallas is one of the team's truly special victories!

The Incredible Reggie White

THE EAGLES HAVE HAD A LOT OF ELITE PLAYERS in their history, but perhaps the very best is a tremendous defensive lineman named Reggie White, who starred with the Birds from 1985 to 1992. Reggie was so great that many experts consider him the best defensive lineman in NFL history! He could play the run and get after quarterbacks with remarkable strength, quickness, and skilled moves. He was also an inspiring figure, and not just because of his on-field dominance. He was an ordained minister who treated people with kindness. Teammates, fans, and media members all loved him. Reggie may have been the most respected NFL player during his time in the league. "The Minister Of Defense" was special!

He had so many accomplishments with the Birds, but his best may have been in 1987 when he almost broke the NFL season sack record of 22 sacks in just 12 games. Across the league in '87, players went on strike in a dispute with owners. As a result, a week of games was canceled, and for three weeks owners even used replacement players. Therefore, Reggie only played 12 games instead of 16. But that did not stop him. Reggie had a sack in all but one of his 12 games! He had two or more sacks in eight games! For the season Reggie had an astounding 21 sacks in just 12 games as he was voted the 1987 NFL Defensive Player of the Year!

He also played a huge role helping turn around the Birds after bad seasons in the mid-80s. Reggie, thrilling QB Randall Cunningham, and fan-favorite coach Buddy Ryan led the way as "Buddy Ball" brought swagger and exciting victories, such as a win over Dallas in '87 with a fake kneel-down that turned into a deep pass, "The Bounty Bowl" in '89 vs. Dallas, and "The Body Bag Game" in '90 vs. Washington! Buddy charged up the town with his outrageous personality, feuds, and tactics to try to win. The Birds made the playoffs four times in Reggie's eight years in Philly, and deepened the team's connection to fans in a big way! Sadly, owner Norman Braman let Reggie go after 1992. When he retired

Perhaps the greatest Eagles player of all-time, Reggie White is often ranked as one of the 10 best players in NFL history. (Tom DiPace/AP Images)

following the 2000 season, Reggie held the NFL's career record with an awesome 198 sacks! Tragically, Reggie died in 2004 at the age of 43. His No. 92 was retired by the Birds in '05, and in '06 he was elected to the Pro Football Hall of Fame. Reggie will always be remembered as one of the most special people and one of the most dominant players to ever play in Philly!

1991 Eagles Defense Ranks No. 1 Across the Board

REGGIE WHITE WAS NOT THE ONLY ELITE DEFENSIVE PLAYER the Eagles acquired during the 1980s as they assembled a terrific group of defenders. Head coach Buddy Ryan brought much of it together through the draft, but after three straight playoff losses the Birds fired Buddy. Fans were unhappy, but the move did help usher in legendary coach Bud Carson as the team's new defensive coordinator.

Using the players Buddy had developed, in 1991 the Eagles defense under Carson turned in one of the most unbelievable performances in NFL history. They were so dominant that the '91 Eagles D is the only defense in the NFL since 1976 to be No. 1 across the board statistically: No. 1 against the rush, No. 1 against the pass, and therefore No. 1 overall in fewest yards allowed! It was a staggering achievement! The accomplishment was all the more remarkable because the Eagles had major issues on offense in '91. Star quarterback Randall Cunningham suffered a season-ending injury in the first game. Even Randall's backup, Jim McMahon, got hurt. The Birds were forced to play with weak quarterbacks (five different QBs started games), and a bad rushing attack (the team's leading rusher had only 440 yards the entire season).

The burden of all of this fell on the Birds defense. With Reggie, Jerome Brown, Clyde Simmons, Mike Pitts, Mike Golic, Seth Joyner,

Byron Evans, William Thomas, Eric Allen, Ben Smith, Wes Hopkins, and Andre Waters, the Birds "Gang Green" defense turned in a season for the ages. They allowed only 71 rushing yards and 151 passing yards per game! They led the league with 48 turnovers and 54 sacks! There were memorable games along the way such as when they shut out Dallas, sacking Troy Aikman 11 times, and the "House of Pain Game" in Houston when Seth was at his all-time best as the Birds held a great Oilers offense to only six points scored!

When the season was over honors and awards rolled in, as Reggie, Jerome, Clyde, Seth, and Eric Allen made the Pro Bowl! Seth was named *Sports Illustrated*'s NFL Player of the Year, with 110 tackles, 6.5 sacks, three interceptions, six forced fumbles, and four fumble recoveries! The '91 Eagles defense is sometimes overlooked in national discussions of the greatest defenses ever because the team went 10–6 and did not make the playoffs. But Philadelphia sports fans who saw them play will always know they are one of the elite defenses in NFL history, and one of the most extraordinary groups in Philly sports history!

Two Thrilling Playoff Victories in the 1990s

FANS LOVED THE BIRDS TEAMS of the late 1980s and early 1990s, which featured an elite defense led by Reggie White, and skilled players such as QB Randall Cunningham, star WR Mike Quick (a sensational five-time Pro Bowler who once caught a 99-yard TD to win a game!), TE Keith Jackson, and RB Keith Byars on offense. Randall ("The Ultimate Weapon") amazed fans with remarkably athletic plays such as when he survived a hit from Carl Banks to throw a TD on *Monday Night Football* in '88, when he punted the ball 91 yards in '89, and in '90 when he escaped Bruce Smith in the endzone to throw a 95-yard TD to Fred Barnett! Sensational plays had become routine, but playoff failure had as well. Entering 1992 the talented Birds had won 10 or more games four years in a row, but had gone 0–3 in the playoffs in that time.

In '92 beloved star Jerome Brown tragically died in a car crash. It was devastating. The team decided they wanted to "Bring It Home For Jerome" that season. When they went 11–5, fans hoped this would finally be the year Randall and Reggie's Eagles would win a playoff game. But for three quarters of a Wild Card game against the Saints, another playoff loss seemed brewing. The Birds trailed 20–10 to start the fourth quarter. Then they got busy thrilling fans with one of the most electrifying quarters in their history. Randall threw a 35-yard TD pass to Barnett! Heath Sherman scored on a six-yard run giving the Eagles the lead! Reggie recorded a safety of the Saints QB! After an Eagles field goal, Eric Allen intercepted a pass and returned it for a TD to clinch the game! Incredibly, the Birds had outscored the Saints 26–0 in the fourth quarter to win their first playoff game in 12 years!

The Eagles lost the next week to Dallas, and over a few years most of the squad's best players left as free agents. Following 8–8 and 7–9 seasons, new owner Jeffrey Lurie hired Ray Rhodes as head coach in 1995. The Birds vastly improved that year with inspired play from a new core, which included Barnett, Ricky Watters, Charlie Garner, and Rodney Peete on offense; and William Fuller, Andy Harmon, William Thomas, Bill Romanowski, and Bobby Taylor on defense. In a key December win, the Birds D famously stopped Dallas' Emmitt Smith twice on fourth-and-1 (only one of them counted)! They made the playoffs with a 10–6 record, but entered the postseason as home underdogs to Detroit. However, in one of the most amazing playoff performances ever, the Birds demolished the Lions, as Peete threw three touchdowns and Watters scored twice! Fans were thrilled as the Birds put up an astounding 58 points in a 58–37 win! The 58 points remains the fourth most points ever scored in an NFL playoff game!

Fourth-and-26

ONLY A COUPLE OF PLAYS OR MOMENTS in Philly sports go by a name. "The Miracle At The Meadowlands," "Jimmy's Double Off Broxton," "Fourth-and-1," "the Shift," "the Philly Special," "Schmidty's 500th Home Run," and "the Double Doink" are all very memorable and special. So is "Fourth-and-26," one of the top moments in Eagles history.

Hopes were high for the 2003 Birds, especially after quality seasons from 2000 to '02 under head coach Andy Reid as the Birds built themselves around the star play of QB Donovan McNabb on offense and safety Brian Dawkins on defense. The '03 Eagles were another great squad, going 12–4, but against Green Bay in their first playoff game at the Linc they were a mess early, falling behind 14–0. The Birds rebounded to tie the score, but in the fourth quarter the Packers took a 17–14 lead. With just two minutes left the Eagles faced their most important drive of the year. If they did not score, their season would be over. On first down, McNabb threw an incomplete pass. On second down, disaster struck as he was sacked for a 16-yard loss. On third-and-26 McNabb threw another incompletion. It would all come down to fourth-and-26. Rarely had a big moment felt more hopeless. Fourth-and-26 felt almost impossible.

With the season on the line, Reid called "74 Double Go," a play designed to get the ball down the field. As McNabb dropped back, Green Bay was in a zone, which meant the middle of the field might just be open. WR Freddie Mitchell, the Birds outspoken former first-round pick, ran right toward the Packers 48-yard line, which is where the Eagles needed to cross to get a first down. As fans at the Linc held their breath, McNabb threw the ball toward Mitchell, who twisted his body and, despite having two Packers around him, caught the ball! He absorbed contact lunging forward! McNabb and "Fred-Ex" had delivered, as Freddie was awarded the first down! The crowd went wild! The Eagles had converted fourth-and-26!

Freddie Mitchell catches the ball on fourth-and-26 to keep the Eagles season alive. (Doug Pensinger/Getty Images)

The Birds still had work to do though. With the clock ticking they moved the ball down the field, and with five seconds left David Akers hit a clutch 37-yard field goal sending the game into overtime! Then in OT, Dawkins intercepted a Brett Favre pass, and returned it 35 yards! Akers followed with another field goal to win the game! Fourth-and-26 will always represent a moment when the Eagles escaped almost certain season-ending doom to somehow, someway find a path to victory!

2004 Eagles Dominate the NFC

FOLLOWING EARLY SUCCESS UNDER RAY RHODES in 1995 and '96, the Birds bottomed out in '98, going 3–13. Rhodes was fired. Jeffrey Lurie and team president Joe Banner, who was instrumental in elevating the franchise, hired Andy Reid as the Birds new coach. That spring, the Eagles rightfully selected Donovan McNabb with the No. 2 overall pick in the draft. And so began the organization's climb as they aimed for a Super Bowl.

The '99 Eagles struggled in Reid and McNabb's first year, but in 2000 the team took off. It all began Week 1 with "the Pickle Juice Game" as players drank pickle juice on a hot day in Dallas while exciting fans by recovering an onside kick to start the season! Duce Staley rushed for 201 yards in the eye-opening win! By year's end, the Birds had an 11–5 record and won a playoff game! They appeared headed toward a very bright future. In 2001 the climb continued as the Eagles went 11–5 and won the NFC East for the first time since 1988! Two playoff wins followed as the Birds reached the NFC Championship Game for the first time since the '80 season! In 2002 they improved again going 12–4 while tying the franchise record for most wins in a season! By this time, Brian Dawkins, on his way to a Hall of Fame career, had become an all-time Philly fan-favorite! One of the NFL's best safeties ever, "Dawk," aka "B-Dawk," aka "Weapon X" was phenomenal! He became the first player ever to have six tackles, a sack, a fumble recovery, an interception, and a 57-yard TD reception (on a fake punt) all in the same game! Despite his and the team's greatness, though, the Birds lost the NFC Championship Game again, this time in heartbreaking fashion in the final football game ever played at The Vet. The Birds managed to come back very strong in '03 with another 12–4 season, but the week after Freddie Mitchell's fourth-and-26 catch helped them beat the Packers in a playoff game, they lost yet again in the NFC title game. Three straight NFC Championship Game losses created major disappointment for fans.

In 2004, with McNabb in his prime and on his way to becoming the franchise's QB record holder for career passing yards, TDs, and wins, the Birds made massive moves to try to climb the mountain. Over the past few years some classic Eagles departed, such as Staley, Troy Vincent, and Bobby Taylor, but Reid and Banner pulled off an incredible off-season, adding star pass rusher Jevon Kearse and star wide receiver Terrell Owens! Plus, they re-signed fan-favorites Jeremiah Trotter and Hugh Douglas! Both had been tremendous for the Birds a few years earlier. Training Camp became packed with fans. The hype was huge! This was a loaded team: McNabb, RB Brian Westbrook, FB Jon Ritchie, "T.O." (Owens), TEs Chad Lewis, and L.J. Smith, an elite offensive line featuring Jon Runyan and Tra Thomas, a fantastic defensive line which included Kearse and Corey Simon, "the Axe Man" (Trotter) at LB, CBs Lito Sheppard and Sheldon Brown, and Dawkins and Michael Lewis at safety! Plus, they had legendary defensive coordinator Jim Johnson, and exceptional special teams under John Harbaugh, which featured Pro Bowlers David Akers and Ike Reese! This squad did not just beat opponents; they destroyed them. McNabb and T.O. were an electric combo, and they showed that Week 1, hooking up for three TDs! By late October, the Birds were an awesome 7–0! After a loss in Pittsburgh, they beat the Cowboys as T.O., on his way to 77 catches for 1,200 yards and 14 touchdowns for the season, had three more TDs in a 49–21 win! After that, the Birds outscored their next three opponents 102–29! In December, with a 13–1 record, the Eagles clinched home-field advantage for the playoffs, but in a blow, lost T.O. to a serious leg and ankle injury. Fans were extremely disappointed as it seemed he would miss the playoffs.

Without T.O., the Eagles needed to win two home games to get over the NFC title game hump. First, they beat Minnesota 27–14! This set up one of the most critical games in Birds history: their fourth straight crack at the NFC Championship Game, this time against Michael Vick and Atlanta. On a very cold day in front of a fired up crowd at the Linc, Jim Johnson's defense played fantastic, containing Vick. Dawk provided perhaps the most memorable moment when he laid out Alge Crumpler

After winning the NFC Championship Game, Andy Reid is interviewed as Donovan McNabb (left), Brian Dawkins, and Terrell Owens (right) take in the moment. (Tomasso DeRosa/AP Images)

with a massive hit! The Birds offense scored two touchdowns, taking a 20–10 lead, and then with 3:21 left the Eagles sealed the victory as Chad Lewis caught his second TD of the game to make it 27–10! Finally, with a thrilling victory, this Eagles group broke through! Fans were full of joy as the Birds were headed to the Super Bowl!

Unfortunately, the Eagles lost Super Bowl XXXIX 24–21 to a great Patriots team, even though T.O. returned from his injury and played incredible, with nine catches for 122 yards. Players and fans still wonder if Patriots coach Bill Belichick robbed the Birds of a Super Bowl by cheating in the game. Regardless, the '04 Eagles provided so much fun for fans during a remarkable season. They are clearly one of Philly's best teams ever!

Making the Playoffs in Dramatic Fashion in 2008

BEING A PHILLY SPORTS FAN INVOLVES A LOT OF HEARTBREAK. From the '64 Phillies ... to the Sixers and Phils playoff losses in '77 ... Joe Carter's home run ... Rhonde Barber's interception ... the Birds three Super Bowl losses ... Kawhi Leonard's shot ... Patrick Kane's goal ... the Phils playoff losses in '22, '23, and '24 ... being a Philly sports fan can be tough.

But every once in a while in the face of very long odds things break right—exactly right—for a Philadelphia team and its fans. This was certainly true on the final day of the 2008 NFL regular season when against all odds the Eagles somehow made the playoffs. Entering the day, the 8–6–1 Birds faced the almost-certain end of their season. For the Eagles to make the playoffs they needed all sorts of help from other teams in the 1:00 PM games. At least two of three things had to occur: the 12–3 Giants beating the 9–6 Vikings in Minnesota; the 7–8 Texans defeating the 9–6 Bears in Houston; the 4–11 Raiders besting the 9–6 Bucs in Tampa. Plus, even if that all happened, the Eagles would still then need to beat a good Cowboys team in their 4:15 PM game at the Linc. Fans were very pessimistic. It seemed so unlikely.

Early in the 1:00 PM games things were terrible: Chicago led the Texans 10–0; the Vikings led the Giants 10–0. It felt hopeless, especially when Tampa had a 10-point, fourth-quarter lead over the Raiders. But in the fourth quarter the Texans scored 10-straight points to take control versus the Bears! Houston went on to win 31–24! Unfortunately, the Vikings beat the Giants, but seemingly out of nowhere the Raiders started coming back vs. Tampa, scoring 17-straight fourth-quarter points! Shockingly, the Raiders, a horrendous team, won 31–24!

Perhaps the most beloved Eagles player ever, Brian Dawkins was a remarkable and inspiring player during his Hall of Fame career. (Brian Garfinkel/AP Images)

As kickoff approached, Birds players and fans at the Linc were thrilled because the Eagles-Cowboys game would be for the final playoff spot! Minutes earlier the game seemed meaningless; now everything was on the line against the Birds' rival! The crowd was pumped! With renewed energy, the Eagles dominated all day. The Birds D, led by Brian Dawkins, forced five Cowboys turnovers and scored twice! The Eagles offense, led by Donovan McNabb, played great on their way to a 44–6 rout! In an unbelievably dramatic turn of events, the Birds were headed to the playoffs!

However, after two great postseason wins, the Eagles lost the NFC Championship Game. The Birds' quest to win their first Super Bowl would continue on a while longer.

The Eagles Finally Win the Super Bowl

FOR MANY YEARS, PERHAPS THE BIGGEST DREAM of Philly sports fans was the hope that the Eagles would win the Super Bowl. They had won three NFL championships, but in the Super Bowl era dating back to the late 1960s, the Birds never won it all—while their NFC East rivals won it 12 times. Fans were desperate for a Super Bowl.

Eight years after falling short in Super Bowl XXXIX, six years after a good playoff run with QB Jeff Garcia in the 2006 season, and a few years removed from playoff appearances in ’08, ’09, and ’10, Andy Reid was fired after a brutal 2012 season. The Birds hired Chip Kelly. He started strong with a team built around Michael Vick, LeSean McCoy, DeSean Jackson, and Brent Celek on offense, and Trent Cole, Fletcher Cox, DeMeco Ryans, and Connor Barwin on defense. The "Snow Bowl," in which LeSean, who eventually would go on to become the franchise's all-time leading rusher, ran wild in the snow with 217 yards versus Detroit, was a highlight! So too was quarterback Nick Foles' play as he stepped in for Vick to lead the Eagles to a playoff berth in ‘13, but Chip's run crumbled in ’15, and he was fired. In ’16 the Eagles went 7–9 with new coach Doug Pederson and rookie QB Carson Wentz. Fans hoped the Birds would make the playoffs the next season, but a special year seemed unlikely. GM Howie Roseman made moves for ’17, and built the team's core around Wentz, offensive linemen Jason Peters, Jason Kelce, Brandon Brooks, and Lane Johnson; tight end Zach Ertz; wide receiver Alshon Jeffery; defensive linemen Cox and Brandon Graham; linebacker Jordan Hicks; and safeties Malcolm Jenkins and Rodney McLeod.

The Eagles got off to a fast start Week 1 as Wentz threw a TD to Nelson Agholor on their first possession. Fans were encouraged as the Birds won their opener. They lost Week 2 in KC against their former coach, Reid, but rebounded Week 3 with their first magical moment as Jake Elliott made a 61-yard field goal to beat the Giants! From there the Birds really took off. Wentz was playing exceptional, and with strength along the offensive and defensive line the Eagles won their next eight games! The team had remarkable chemistry. Fans were thinking Super Bowl!

But big injuries set in along the way. Kicker Caleb Sturgis, RB Darren Sproles, Peters, Hicks, and special teams ace Chris Maragos all suffered season-ending injuries. After losing to Seattle, disaster struck Week 14, as Wentz severely injured his knee trying to dive for a touchdown. Incredibly, Wentz stayed in to finish the drive with a TD pass, but he then had to leave the game as Foles, who had been reacquired by Howie before the season, went in. The Birds pulled it out with Foles to beat the Rams and clinch the NFC East, but fans were devastated that Wentz, the frontrunner for the MVP Award, would miss the rest of the season. Almost everyone thought the Eagles chances of winning the Super Bowl had taken a huge hit. But after the game Jenkins set the tone for his squad the rest of the season with a motivational speech, in which he said, "We all we got. We all we need."

Fans were familiar with Foles since he had been the Birds starting QB for parts of 2012, 2013 (27 TDs and 2 INTs, a seven-TD game, Pro Bowl MVP) and 2014, but in 2017's last two regular season games he struggled a lot. Oddsmakers doubted Foles and the Birds. Despite going 13–3, the Eagles entered the postseason as a home underdog to Atlanta. The Birds now had an underdog rallying cry! Against the Falcons, the Eagles offense struggled somewhat, but the Birds D played fantastic. With just 1:05 left in the fourth quarter the Eagles held a 15–10 lead. The Falcons had fourth-and-goal from the 2-yard line, but the Birds kept Atlanta from scoring, as Falcons star Julio Jones was unable to catch a potential TD! The Birds won, and were headed to the NFC Championship Game! Lane Johnson and Chris Long wore dog masks after the game as players showed they embraced the underdog role!

In the NFC Championship Game the Eagles were again home underdogs, and they struggled early as Minnesota took a 7–0 lead. But in one of the year's most critical plays, Long disrupted a pass, and Patrick Robinson intercepted the ball, returning it 50 yards for a TD! From that point on the Birds absolutely crushed Minnesota! Foles was sensational, with three TDs, including two to Jeffery and one to Torrey Smith on a flea-flicker! With a 38–7 win, the Eagles were headed to the Super Bowl!

On **February 4, 2018,** the Eagles squared off against Tom Brady, Bill Belichick, and the five-time Super Bowl–champion New England Patriots in Super Bowl LII in Minnesota. This was a rematch of sorts, as New England had defeated the 2004 Eagles in Super Bowl XXXIX. Once again the Eagles were underdogs. The Birds came out strong on offense in their first possession, but settled for a field goal. New England responded with their own field goal, tying the game 3–3. The second time the Birds had the ball, Foles connected with Jeffery, who made a spectacular leaping catch for a 34-yard touchdown! On the Eagles' fourth possession, running back LeGarrett Blount rumbled 21 yards for another TD, giving the Birds a 15–3 lead! After nine straight points by New England, the Eagles answered late in the first half as rookie running back Corey Clement caught a short pass and turned it into a 55-yard gain, setting up one of the most shocking and incredible plays in Eagles history: "the Philly Special."

In a fourth-and-goal shocker, Nick Foles scores a touchdown on the Philly Special. (Mike Ehrmann/Getty Images)

During a timeout, with the Birds set to go for fourth-and-goal from the 1-yard line, Foles asked Pederson, "Do you want Philly Philly?" Pederson responded, "Yeah, let's do it." With 38 seconds left in the half, Clement took a direct snap and flipped the ball to tight end Trey Burton, who then passed it to Foles in the end zone for a thrilling TD! The Eagles had a 22–12 halftime lead!

The second half was a roller-coaster of emotions for Eagles fans. Patriots star Rob Gronkowski scored a TD three minutes into the half. Foles responded with a big TD pass to Clement! The Pats followed with another TD, as Brady picked apart the Birds' defense. After an Elliott field goal, Gronk scored another TD, giving New England a 33–32 lead. Foles and the Eagles offense then answered with their most important drive of the season, which included a crucial fourth-and-1 pass to Ertz with five minutes to go, and ended with a TD pass to Ertz for a 38–33 lead with 2:21 left in the game! On the Patriots next drive, in one of the most dramatic moments in Philly sports history, Brandon Graham stripped the ball from Brady, and Derek Barnett recovered it! Elliott followed with a critical field goal for a 41–33 lead!

The Birds D had to stop Brady once more, but he quickly got in position to throw a Hail Mary. With every fan nervous, legendary announcer

Making what many consider the most important play in Eagles history, Brandon Graham (No. 55) strips the ball from Tom Brady late in the fourth quarter of Super Bowl LII. (Streeter Lecka/Getty Images)

Merrill Reese called the action on SportsRadio 94WIP: "What a game. We will never forget this. Hopefully with joy in our hearts. Nine seconds left. Eagles by eight. Brady lines them up … he's back again … he steps up … he's hit … he stumbles … he is throwing it deep for the endzone … and it is … batted around … and … incomplete! And the game is over! The game is over! The Philadelphia Eagles are Super Bowl champions! Eagles fans everywhere, this is for you! Let the celebration begin!" The Birds had *finally* won the Super Bowl! Fans' dream had come true! Foles was named Super Bowl MVP for his amazing performance with 373 passing yards, three TDs thrown, and one TD caught! Jeffrey Lurie, the first to hoist the Lombardi Trophy, said the victory meant "everything" to Philadelphia!

Days later the celebration continued with a parade, as Kelce, on his way to becoming an icon and future Hall of Famer, gave an epic speech about the Eagles and Philly both being a bunch of underdogs and a bunch of "hungry dogs" who overcame so much to win it all! With perhaps the best win in Philly's history, the Eagles were Super Bowl champions!

"Hungry Dogs Run Faster!" Jason Kelce moves into legendary status as he caps the Eagles first Super Bowl victory with an epic parade speech. (Alex Brandon/AP Images)

Birds Soar in 2022

FOLLOWING THEIR SUPER BOWL WIN IN THE 2017 SEASON, the Eagles went backward. Despite another solid playoff push the following year when Nick Foles replaced Carson Wentz again, that 9–7 season and another 9–7 season in 2019 did not duplicate the magic of 2017. Things then totally fell apart in 2020, as the Birds went 4–11–1. Following the season, Doug Pederson was fired and Wentz was traded.

In 2021 the Eagles made the playoffs with second-year QB Jalen Hurts and first-year head coach Nick Sirianni. But after a bad playoff loss fans questioned if the Birds would be elite again soon. However, GM Howie Roseman had a plan. With new additions over a few years such as A.J. Brown, DeVonta Smith, Dallas Goedert, Miles Sanders, Jordan Mailata, Landon Dickerson, Javon Hargrave, Haason Reddick, TJ Edwards, Darius Slay, James Bradbury, and C.J. Gardner-Johnson teaming up with Hurts and stars still around from the 2017 Super Bowl season such as Jason Kelce, Lane Johnson, Fletcher Cox, and Brandon Graham, suddenly the 2022 Eagles were loaded with talent.

In Week 1 the Eagles got by Detroit 38–35. In Week 2 they impressed, beating the Vikings 24–7. From there the Birds began to soar. They won their next six games, upping their record to 8–0 for the first time in franchise history! Hurts was tremendous, with dynamic play as a passer and runner, and the Birds defense was mauling teams! After a Week 10 loss, the Eagles responded with another five-game winning streak! When the regular season was over, the Birds stood atop the NFC standings with a 14–3 record! The defense was second in the league in fewest yards allowed, and registered an amazing 70 sacks, third most in NFL history!

In the divisional round of the playoffs the Birds destroyed the Giants 38–7! In the NFC Championship Game they crushed the 49ers 31–7, as Sanders scored two TDs, and Reddick absolutely manhandled San Fran all day, thrilling fans at the Linc! This win was particularly satisfying as the 49ers were a great team, but they did not seem to truly respect the Birds. The Eagles were headed back to the Super Bowl!

Unfortunately, the Birds lost Super Bowl LVII in very disappointing fashion to Andy Reid, Patrick Mahomes, and the Kansas City Chiefs. Despite this, the 2022 Eagles, who totally dominated the NFC, are easily one of the very best Birds teams ever!

Saquon Barkley's Extraordinary Season Helps the Eagles Leap to the Top Again

FOLLOWING THEIR LOSS IN SUPER BOWL LVII, the Eagles had a very odd season in 2023. A tremendous 10–1 start raised Super Bowl hopes again, but a historic collapse followed as the Birds lost six of their final seven games. It was all so strange. How could a team that had gone 26–5 during 2022 (including playoffs) and a portion of 2023 suddenly and so dramatically lose their way? Questions swirled about head coach Nick Sirianni and QB Jalen Hurts. The team's defense needed to be rebuilt. Fans were disgusted. GM Howie Roseman set out on a critical off-season to try to right the Eagles ship.

Howie's 2024 off-season ranks amongst the very best in Philly sports history. The club brought in two accomplished coordinators: Kellen Moore to run the offense, and veteran Vic Fangio to oversee the defense. Howie drafted cornerbacks Quinyon Mitchell and Cooper DeJean. He signed defenders Zack Baun and C.J. Gardner-Johnson, as well as offensive lineman Mekhi Becton. And for his biggest move of all, Howie signed a player away from the rival Giants. His name: Saquon Barkley!

These players joined a squad that kept much of its offensive core from 2023 together: QB Jalen Hurts, WRs A.J. Brown and DeVonta Smith, TE Dallas Goedert, and linemen Jordan Mailata, Landon Dickerson, Cam Jurgens, and Lane Johnson. On defense, veteran stars Brandon Graham and Darius Slay remained in the fold, but the unit would also lean on less-proven returning younger players such as Jalen Carter, Josh Sweat, Jordan Davis, Milton Williams, Nolan Smith, Nakobe Dean, and Reed Blankenship. Plus, the Birds would have to overcome the loss of Jason Kelce and Fletcher Cox, who had both recently retired, and of Haason Reddick, who had been traded. The Eagles were projected by many fans to be a playoff team, but after the collapse in 2023, a truly special season in 2024 seemed unlikely.

In Week 1, Saquon's impact was immediate; he scored three TDs versus Green Bay as the Birds won the first NFL game ever played in Brazil! But then the Eagles struggled, losing two of their next three games to fall to 2–2. Even after a Week 6 win, fans were frustrated as the Birds barely got by a bad Browns team. Sirianni was facing criticism. But the Eagles picked it up Week 7, as Saquon excelled against his former team with 176 yards rushing! The Birds cruised to a 28–3 win over New York. While questions remained about how good the team was overall, two realities had come into focus: Saquon was sensational, and the Eagles defense was much better than anticipated!

In Week 9, the Birds got by the lowly Jags 28–23 to up their record to 6–2 as Dean made a game-saving interception to seal the win! But this game will always be remembered primarily for one thing: Saquon's backward leap, one of the most exceptional plays in NFL history! In an extraordinary and utterly shocking play, Saquon, after catching a pass in the flat from Hurts, ran through one defender, did a spin move to get past another, and then jumped backward over a third defender before finishing forward with power as two other defenders finally brought him down! Never before had anyone seen anything like this! After six years of honorable toil with a horrendous Giants franchise, halfway through his first season in Philly, Saquon put America on notice of his true greatness!

The Birds followed that up with a 34–6 destruction of Dallas as Hurts passed for two TDs and ran for another two TDs! The Tush Push with Hurts was all but unstoppable, as he would use his strength to convert short-yardage plays behind the power and technique of Jurgens,

In a play for the ages, Saquon Barkley leaps over a Jaguars defender backward. (Chris Szagola/AP Images)

Dickerson, and Mailata along the left side of the offensive line. After defeating Washington, the Eagles season got even more exciting as they posted very impressive back-to-back road wins at the Rams and at the Ravens! In LA, Saquon was at his all-time best, running for an astounding 255 yards and two TDs, while also catching four passes for another 47 yards! In Baltimore, the Birds defense shut down stars Lamar Jackson and Derrick Henry! DeJean made one of the top plays of the year by stopping Henry in his tracks, lifting him up, and slamming the massive running back hard to the ground! At 10–2, fans were pumped!

In Week 14 the Birds clinched a playoff spot by defeating Carolina as Saquon rushed for another 124 yards to break LeSean McCoy's single-season club rushing record of 1,607 yards! With four regular season games left, Saquon had a legitimate shot to break Eric Dickerson's all-time regular season rushing record of 2,105 yards. In Week 15, Hurts played perhaps his best regular season game as he threw for 290 yards and two TDs, while running for 45 yards and another TD, as the Eagles handled Pittsburgh 27–13! Week 17, playing without an injured Hurts, the Birds crushed the Cowboys 41–7 as Saquon ran for 167 yards to become just the ninth player in league history to rush for 2,000 yards in a season! It was a spectacular accomplishment for Saquon! Fans at the Linc showered him with a huge ovation as they showed their appreciation for his remarkable season! It was also a spectacular accomplishment for the team's offensive line, whom Saquon was quick to praise. Mailata, Dickerson, Jurgens, Becton, and Johnson had dominated up front all season! They had been guided every step of the way by Jeff Stoutland, the squad's legendary offensive line coach. With a shot for Saquon to break Dickerson's record Week 18, Sirianni decided it was in the team's best interest to rest the star running back and most of the starters, since the Birds were locked in as the NFC's No. 2 seed for the playoffs. Saquon and the team knew there was a bigger goal in mind: winning the Super Bowl.

The regular season had been a massive success. At 14–3, which included a club-record 10-straight wins, the Eagles tied their franchise mark for most regular season wins! They formed a special bond with each other in large part due to the outstanding coaching of Sirianni, who consistently preached messages of "Tough, detailed, together," and "You can't be great without the greatness of others." Saquon, in one of the most extraordinary seasons in Philly sports history, finished with an astounding 2,005 yards rushing! Hurts had 18 TD passes, only five interceptions, and a passer rating of 103.7! He also ran for 630 yards and an awesome 14 TDs on the ground! The defense finished No. 1 in the NFL for fewest yards allowed for the first time since the Birds' legendary Gang Green unit from 1991! Along the way, Carter, Baun, Mitchell, and DeJean emerged as defensive stars! Saquon and Baun were named First Team All-Pros, while Brown, Mailata, Johnson, and Carter all earned Second Team All-Pro honors! Plus, Baun finished fifth for Defensive Player of the Year, and Saquon was named the Offensive Player of the

Year (although he should have won MVP)! The Birds were ready for the playoffs.

In the Wild Card round versus Green Bay, Saquon had a big day on the ground with 119 rushing yards, Goedert showed brute force on a catch-and-run TD, and the defense played fantastic against Jordan Love, as the Eagles won 22–10!

In the divisional round versus the Rams, Hurts got the scoring going early with a tremendous 44-yard TD run, and Saquon added a TD of 62 yards, and another of 78 yards as he dashed through the snow on a beautiful, wintry night in Philly to seemingly put the Rams away as the crowd at the Linc went wild! But LA responded with a quick touchdown, and were threatening again deep in Eagles territory late in the fourth quarter. Fans were nervous as the season hung in the balance. Carter then stepped up with perhaps the two most important plays of the entire year as he sacked Matthew Stafford on third down, and forced an incompletion on fourth down! With a 28–22 win, the Birds were headed to the NFC Championship Game!

In the conference title game, they faced Jayden Daniels and Washington at the Linc. The Commanders had upset Detroit the prior week, giving the Eagles home-field advantage for the big matchup. On the Birds' first play from scrimmage, Saquon electrified the crowd with yet another iconic moment, scoring on a thrilling 60-yard run! While the game was close for most of the first half, the Eagles eventually took control in a very big way. The Birds' defense forced four turnovers, Saquon added two more touchdowns, and Hurts played absolutely superb with a touchdown through the air and three TDs on the ground as the Eagles destroyed Washington 55–23! The Birds were headed to the Super Bowl for just the fifth time in franchise history!

In a rematch from Super Bowl LVII, the Eagles entered Super Bowl LIX in New Orleans as a slight underdog to Andy Reid, Patrick Mahomes, and the back-to-back defending-champion Kansas City Chiefs, who were aiming to become the first team to win three straight Super Bowls. But on **February 9, 2025,** the Chiefs basically had no chance because of the elite roster Howie had assembled, and because of the superior way Sirianni's team played. Hurts got the Birds on the board with a Tush Push TD! Jake Elliott followed with a field goal to make it 10–0! Fangio's defense was dominating Mahomes as Sweat, Carter, Williams, Smith, BG, and others brought relentless pressure up front, while the linebackers and secondary played exceptional in coverage! In the second quarter, DeJean (on his birthday) made a spectacular play, picking off Mahomes and running 38 yards for a defensive touchdown! Fans were elated, and that feeling continued shortly before the half as Baun intercepted another Mahomes pass, and two plays later Hurts hit A.J. Brown with a 12-yard touchdown, putting the Eagles up 24–0! After another defensive stop, the Birds got the ball back shortly before halftime. On the final play of the half, Saquon ran for two yards. It was a simple run as the offense ran out the clock, taking a 24–0 lead into the locker room, but with this run Saquon achieved another remarkable feat as he passed Hall of Famer Terrell Davis to set the NFL record for

Cooper Dejean's interception returned for a touchdown on his birthday was one of many amazing highlights for the Eagles during their blowout of the Chiefs in Super Bowl LIX. (Doug Benc/AP Images)

the most combined regular season and postseason rushing yards in one year!

In the second half, the rout continued. An Elliott field goal made it 27–0, and then after a terrific fourth-down pass defense by Avonte Maddox, Hurts, on his way to winning the Super Bowl MVP Award with an absolutely dominant performance through the air and on the ground, hit DeVonta Smith with a 46-yard bomb to put the Eagles up 34–0! The Birds finally started to ease up once the score was 40–6, as Sirianni put in a lot of the backups. As the game wound down, everyone knew the Eagles had put together one of the best Super Bowl performances of all time! This was tremendous redemption for Sirianni and Hurts who had been doubted by so many both locally and nationally. It was also

Jalen Hurts flashes a big smile after his sensational MVP performance in Super Bowl LIX. (Cooper Neill/Getty Images)

redemption for the entire team after the collapse in 2023. The Birds had proven themselves to be one of the most mentally tough and physically tough teams ever! In the game's final seconds, legendary announcer Merrill Reese called the action on SportsRadio 94WIP: "Ten, nine, eight, seven, six, five, four, three, two, one ... it's over! The Philadelphia Eagles have won Super Bowl LIX! They have beaten the Kansas City Chiefs 40–22! It's their second Super Bowl win in seven years! What a game! What a season! What a team! The greatest Eagles team in modern history! Eagles fans, savor it, and rejoice!"

And rejoice fans did five days later with an enormous parade through Philly which culminated at the Rocky Steps in front of the Art Museum! The town had tremendous appreciation for Jeffrey Lurie and Howie, who together became Philadelphia's first owner/GM duo to win two titles in the past 50 years! Brandon Graham, one of four players to win Super Bowl LII and Super Bowl LIX, gave his parade speech with both Lombardi Trophies right in front of him! With their monumental season, which included immensely impressive performances in both the NFC Championship Game and the Super Bowl, there are some who believe the 2024 Eagles were the very best team in the history of Philadelphia sports!

THE BIG FIVE

Tom Gola Shines as La Salle Wins the 1954 NCAA Championship

COLLEGE BASKETBALL IS A MAJOR PART OF SPORTS in America, and no city may have a better tradition of college hoops than Philadelphia, which is home to six Division 1 schools. Each of Philly's traditional Big 5 teams (La Salle, Penn, Temple, St. Joe's, and Villanova) plus Drexel have had great moments, including when the Dragons won an NCAA Tournament game in 1996 with standout Malik Rose. Many Big 5 games have been played at the legendary Palestra, one of the greatest venues for sports anywhere in America.

La Salle has had some tremendous players through the years such as Ken Durrett, Michael Brooks, and Lionel Simmons. Playing for Speedy Morris, Simmons, the "L-Train," is fifth all-time in points scored in men's college hoops! But no Explorer ever shined more than Tom Gola in 1954 when La Salle won the NCAA championship. Playing for coach Ken Loeffler, the junior star excelled, averaging 23 points and 21.7 rebounds per game! Other Explorers contributed such as Charles Singley, Frank Blatcher, and Frank O'Hara. In the regular season La Salle went 21–4 to qualify for the NCAA Tournament. In the first round they trailed Fordham by two points with just five seconds left, but Gola assisted on a Frank O'Malley bucket with one second to go, forcing overtime! In OT the Explorers won 76–74! In the second round Gola and Stingley each scored 26 points in an 88–81 win over NC State! La Salle next handled Navy 64–48 as Gola scored 22 points, helping the Explorers advance to the semifinals (what we now call the Final Four)! In the semis, Gola and Blatcher each scored 19 points as La Salle defeated Penn State 69–54 to advance to the title game!

On **March 20, 1954,** La Salle faced Bradley in the championship game in Kansas City, Missouri. At halftime Bradley led 43–42, but in the second half La Salle took control. Blatcher and Singley each scored

23 points, and Gola added 19 points and 19 rebounds as La Salle pulled away for a 92–76 win to capture the championship! Gola was named the tournament's Most Outstanding Player! After finishing his amateur career in 1955 as college basketball's all-time leading rebounder (a record he still holds), Gola went on to a 10-year NBA career, which included six seasons and a title with the Philadelphia Warriors! He later coached La Salle for two seasons. Gola's 1969 squad was a force, going 23–1 with Durrett starring! Gola was inducted into the Naismith Memorial Basketball Hall of Fame in 1976!

Penn Makes the 1979 NCAA Final Four

THE UNIVERSITY OF PENNSYLVANIA IS ONE OF THE TOP academic schools in the country, and while Penn has had some success in the Ivy League and in the Big 5, the Quakers have not been a traditional power in college basketball. Ivy League schools do not award athletic scholarships. That makes it very hard to recruit the best players. Despite this, Penn has had notable teams through the years, such as Fran Dunphy's 1994 squad with Jerome Allen and Matt Maloney that won an NCAA Tournament game. But it is Penn's 1979 team under coach Bob Weinhauer that most energized fans as they stunned everyone by making it to the Final Four.

The '79 squad knew how to win in part because Penn had won often in the 1970s. Entering the season, the Quakers had won seven of the previous nine Ivy League crowns and six of the past nine Big 5 titles. So when they played great in '79, going 13–1 in the Ivy League and 3–1 in the Big 5, it was not a shock. However, what happened in the NCAA Tournament was a very big shock … and a very big thrill.

Led by forward Tony Price, who averaged 19.8 points and 8.7 rebounds, the Quakers entered the tournament knowing they would face tough competition. As a No. 9 seed they were expected to win one game at most. In the first round Penn got by No. 8 Iona 73–69. In the second round they played a true national power, Dean Smith's No. 1 seeded North Carolina Tar Heels. With 25 points from Price, in a shocking game, the Quakers beat UNC 72–71 to advance to the Sweet 16! In the third round Penn defeated fourth-seeded Syracuse 84–76 to advance to the Elite Eight! With a chance to go to the Final Four, facing No. 10 seed St. John's, Price led the Quakers with 21 points, as Penn survived a back-and-forth game to win 64–62! Unbelievably, Penn was headed to the Final Four!

In the Final Four, two games away from winning the national championship, the Quakers finally lost to Magic Johnson and the Michigan State Spartans, as Magic controlled the game on his way to basketball superstardom. It was a tough end, but Penn and Philly hoops fans were extremely proud of what the Quakers had accomplished! With talent and determination, and by winning four games in the tournament, Penn, the Big 5 and Ivy League school from Philly with no athletic scholarships, proved they could compete with the very best in college basketball!

Freshman Mark Macon and Coach John Chaney Lead Temple to No. 1 in the Land

TEMPLE HAS ENJOYED STRONG college basketball success throughout many decades. Over the years the Owls have had many quality players and great teams that have made trips to the NCAA Tournament. In the 1950s they reached the national semifinals twice, with Guy Rodgers starring on both squads, and Hal Lear starring alongside Rodgers on one of them. In more modern times, the 1988 team stands out as Temple's best squad of the past 50 years. In fact, they were so good Temple was ranked No. 1 in the nation in '88 for over a month!

John Chaney had a lot of fire and a lot of wisdom during his 24 years as coach of Temple. (Joseph Labolito/Getty Images)

As the season approached, coach John Chaney knew freshman guard Mark Macon would be joining Howie Evans, Mike Vreeswyk, Tim Perry, and Ramon Rivas to form the Owls starting five. Macon made an immediate impact scoring 22 points in his first game leading Temple to a victory over traditional power UCLA. Then the Owls rattled off 13 straight wins to begin the season 14–0! After losing to UNLV by just one point, Temple won four more in a row to become the nation's No. 1 ranked team! The Owls then faced Big 5 rival Villanova in a classic showdown at McGonigle Hall. Temple and Nova battled, but in the end the Owls won 98–86 as Macon scored 31! Temple was now 19–1, and had gone 4–0 in the Big 5! After two more victories, the Owls faced mighty North Carolina on the road in the Dean Dome. Macon and his teammates, particularly Vreeswyk with 26 points, put on an incredible display, absolutely tearing apart UNC with a convincing 83–66 win!

Following the UNC game, Temple won another seven in a row to enter the NCAA Tournament with an unbelievable 29–1 record! The Owls were the No. 1 seed in the East. They easily beat Lehigh, Georgetown, and Richmond to reach the Elite Eight for the first time under Chaney! Unfortunately, with a chance to go to the Final Four, Temple lost to an outstanding Duke team 63–53. It was a disappointing end, but Temple's phenomenal 32–2 season made all Owls fans proud.

The '88 Owls are one of Philly's best college teams ever. Macon averaged 20.6 points, 5.6 rebounds, 2.9 assists, and 1.8 steals! Chaney won the nation's Coach of the Year Award, and would go on to coach Temple for 24 seasons, leading the Owls to 516 wins and a remarkable five trips to the Elite Eight ('88, '91, '93, '99, and '01)! He was inducted into the Basketball Hall of Fame in 2001! Chaney will always be remembered as one of Philly's greatest coaches and truly special people!

Jameer Nelson, Phil Martelli, and St. Joe's Perfect Regular Season

ST. JOE'S HAS HAD VARIOUS MEMORABLE TEAMS through the years, including Jimmy Lynam's 1981 squad, which shocked top-ranked DePaul in the NCAA Tournament with a layup by John Smith at the buzzer on their way to the Elite Eight! But it is the 2004 Hawks that are most legendary in school history. Coached by Phil Martelli, St. Joe's was sensational as they became one of the nation's best teams.

Entering the season, hopes were high with star guard Jameer Nelson returning as a senior, and with the Hawks ranked 17th in the preseason poll. But even the most optimistic fan had no idea how great the ride ahead would be. It all started with a win over Gonzaga. By New Year's, St. Joe's was 10–0 as Jameer and Delonte West dominated in the backcourt, and Pat Carroll, Dwayne Jones, John Bryant, Tyrone Barley, and Chet Stachitas all contributed in big ways. St. Joe's was tearing through their schedule, and in early February they beat La Salle to finish 4–0 in Big 5 play! The Hawks were 20–0 and ranked third in the country! St Joe's fever had taken off in Philly! Then an amazing thing happened as Jameer and St. Joe's were featured on the cover of *Sports Illustrated*, which for decades had been America's premier sports magazine. The headline read: "MEET JAMEER NELSON: THE LITTLE MAN FROM THE LITTLE SCHOOL THAT'S BEATING EVERYONE." This was the first time St. Joe's had made the cover of *SI*! Fans were so proud! The Hawks then won another seven in a row to finish the regular season a perfect 27–0! For the first time ever St. Joe's was ranked No. 1 in the nation!

In the Atlantic 10 Tournament, St. Joe's lost to Xavier, but the Hawks still earned a No. 1 seed in the NCAA Tournament. In the first round they beat Liberty. In the second round they got by Bobby Knight and Texas Tech to advance to the Sweet 16! Then they defeated Wake Forest as Jameer outplayed Chris Paul, leading the Hawks into the Elite Eight!

Phil Martelli (left) and Jameer Nelson (right) put together an incredible season on Hawk Hill in 2004. (Stephan Savoia/AP Images)

However, in a heartbreaker with a chance to go to the Final Four, St. Joe's lost at the very end to Oklahoma State 64–62. It was a very tough defeat. But the season had been an extraordinary success with a record of 30–2 as Martelli was named the National Coach of the Year and Jameer was named the National Player of the Year, averaging 20.6 points, 5.3 assists, 4.7 rebounds, and 2.8 steals! The little school that could, St. Joe's, had risen to No. 1 in the nation, and in the process captured the hearts of people in Philly and all around America!

Villanova Plays a Game for the Ages Under Rollie Massimino ... and Wins Two More Titles Years Later with Jay Wright

OF EVERYTHING THAT HAS HAPPENED IN PHILLY SPORTS, Villanova's 1985 college basketball national championship is one of the most stunning and amazing things ever. In the '85 title game Nova played spectacularly, pulling off one of the most thrilling upsets in sports history by defeating Georgetown 66–64 to win the title. Georgetown, an exceptional team, was considered one of the very best squads of all time. They had the nation's top player, Patrick Ewing, and were the defending champs. The odds were heavily stacked against the Wildcats going into the game.

But Nova coach Rollie Massimino believed his team could win. With seniors Ed Pinckney, Dwayne McClain, and Gary McLain, plus junior Harold Pressley and sophomore Harold Jensen, Nova was battle-tested in the Big East. As a NCAA Tournament No. 8 seed, they made a fantastic run just getting to the Final Four beating No. 9 Dayton, No. 1 Michigan, No. 5 Maryland, and No. 2 North Carolina! In the Final Four they defeated another No. 2 seed, Memphis State, advancing to the title game! However, to win it all they would have to beat the ultimate

No. 1, Ewing's Georgetown Hoyas, their Big East rival. To do that, many thought Nova would have to play almost perfect.

On **April 1, 1985,** in Lexington, Kentucky, Nova and Georgetown battled, with both teams playing phenomenal. In the first half Ewing jammed three straight alley-oop dunks, but each time Villanova responded immediately by scoring. It was David versus Goliath, and Villanova, playing the part of David, was competing well, leading 29–28 at the half! In the second half, playing against one of the top defenses in the nation, Nova used a patient approach, controlling the clock while shooting an amazing nine of 10 from the field! For the game the Wildcats shot a championship-record 78.6 percent from the field! With 2:35 left, Jensen made a huge shot, giving Nova a 55–54 lead! In the next two and a half minutes more baskets and free throws followed, and with just two seconds left Nova held a 66–64 lead! After a timeout, Jensen inbounded the ball to Dwayne McClain, who caught it while lying on the floor, and without travelling secured the ball, yelling excitedly as the clock ticked down … 02 … 01 … 00! With that, CBS announcer Brent Musburger exclaimed: "That's it … Villanova has done it!" Indeed they had! Nova fans everywhere celebrated one of the biggest upsets ever! Villanova was the 1985 national champion!

Incredibly, Villanova's '85 title is not the only championship in school history, as years later the Wildcats under coach Jay Wright won two more national titles! Wright came to Nova in 2001 hoping to restore the program to glory. In '09 they got back to the Final Four on a great Scottie Reynolds basket, but lost in the semis to North Carolina. Wright continued looking for the right pieces to build a title team.

In 2016, Wright and the Wildcats put it all together. With senior Ryan Arcidiacono and junior Josh Hart leading the way, and with Kris Jenkins, Daniel Ochefu, Jalen Brunson, Phil Booth, and Mikal Bridges, Nova entered the tournament as a No. 2 seed with a 29–5 record. In the tournament they easily won their first three games, and then slugged it out in the Elite Eight defeating Kansas to advance to the Final Four! In the semifinal game the Wildcats demolished Oklahoma 95–51 setting up the national championship game against the mighty North Carolina Tar Heels!

On **April 4, 2016,** Villanova and UNC competed in one of the most epic title games in college sports history. With the great Michael Jordan cheering on the Tar Heels and former Nova coach Rollie Massimino cheering on the Wildcats, the game was close for a while, but with five minutes left, Villanova took a 10 point lead! They seemed in control, but then UNC got hot down the stretch, tying it up with 4.7 seconds left. Nova called timeout as Wright set up a play that could win the Wildcats the title. After the timeout, Jenkins inbounded the ball to Arcidiacono who dribbled up-court, and then passed the ball back to Jenkins while Arcidiacono screened Jenkins' defender. With one second left, Jenkins rose up and shot a deep three-pointer as everyone held their breath watching the basketball sail through the air … and go right into the basket! Jenkins swished the shot! It was stunning! Villanova won the national championship on a buzzer beater!

Kris Jenkins launches the only championship game buzzer-beater in the history of the men's NCAA Tournament. (David J. Phillip/AP Images)

Remarkably, with Wright on his way to a Hall of Fame career as one of Philadelphia's best coaches ever, Nova came back two years later and won the title again! Led by Brunson, the National Player of the Year, plus Bridges, Omari Spellman, Eric Paschall, Donte DiVincenzo, and Booth, Villanova played great all year on their way to a final record of 36–4! In the tournament they dominated, winning every game by 12 points or more! On **April 2, 2018,** the Wildcats easily defeated Michigan 79–62 to win the national championship! The Villanova Wildcats, from the Big East and the Big 5, for the third time were at the top of college basketball!

ADDITIONAL

MOMENTS AND STORIES

The Penn Relays

ONE OF PHILADELPHIA'S GREAT SPORTING EVENTS is the Penn Relays, which since the late 1800s has brought together athletes each spring on the campus of the University of Pennsylvania for what has become America's oldest and largest track-and-field competition. From world-class athletes to those at much lower levels, the Penn Relays entertain Philly sports fans and those that travel from around the country and world to see this major annual event.

The Penn Relays began all the way back in 1895 with about 5,000 fans in attendance at the first event ever held at Franklin Field. That year, Harvard defeated Penn in the 4x100 meter relay race, a relatively new race the Penn Relays helped popularize. In 1910, with the growth of the races, the official name of the event was changed to The Penn Relay Carnival. In 1914 it became an international competition, as England's Oxford University participated. Beginning in 1925 winners received a medal or plaque with the likeness of Ben Franklin seated in a chair holding a laurel spring in his left hand as he greets four runners. Over time, more track-and-field events were added to the competition, including the 100-meter dash, hurdles, high jump, pole vault, long jump, decathlon, shot put, hammer throw, javelin, the marathon, and more. In 1962 women competed in the Penn Relays for the first time.

With numerous records set at the Penn Relays through the years, many of the very best track-and-field athletes have competed here, including Jim Thorpe, Jesse Owens, Roger Bannister, Willye White, Bob Beamon, Edwin Moses, Carl Lewis, Leroy Burrell, Michael Johnson, Marion Jones, Usain Bolt, and others! Owens' appearance is particularly meaningful, as he won three events shortly before winning four gold medals in the 1936 Summer Olympics in Berlin! Even individuals famous for other accomplishments have competed in the Penn Relays, such as astronaut Buzz Aldrin, Wilt Chamberlain, longtime Yankees owner George Steinbrenner, politician Bernie Sanders, and actor Luke Wilson!

The Penn Relays are a tremendous source of pride for the University of Pennsylvania and for our city! Some year you should go to Franklin Field in late April to take in this wonderful event!

The Army-Navy Game

ONE OF THE MOST UNIQUE ASPECTS of Philadelphia's sports culture is our town's association with college football's Army-Navy game. In a rivalry that pits two of the United States Armed Forces football programs in a clash of sport, the Army-Navy game has been played almost every year since 1890! Beginning in 1899, when Philly was selected to host the game because of our importance as a city and because we are almost equal distance from Army in West Point, New York, and Navy in Annapolis, Maryland, Philadelphia has hosted this American classic 90 times! Four legendary venues have been used: Franklin Field, Municipal Stadium (later named John Fitzgerald Kennedy Stadium), Veterans Stadium, and Lincoln Financial Field.

The game is so meaningful because players from Army and Navy have made the courageous decision to join our nation's military knowing they may have to fight in war someday. This is no joke. The stakes could not be higher for these young men. There is a totally different level of commitment and sacrifice from students at military schools than from civilian schools, and this is appreciated and respected by millions of Americans! So when the Cadets of Army and Midshipmen of Navy play in the final regular season game each college football season, millions tune in, as they have been doing on radio since 1930 and on TV since 1945.

Despite Army having won three national championships (in 1914, 1944, and 1945), and having won "the Game of the Century" over the

Midshipmen soon after the end of World War II in 1945, Navy leads the series with a 63–55–7 record. Through the years, many star players have played in the game, including Heisman Trophy winners Glenn Davis of Army, and Joe Bellino and Roger Staubach of Navy. Many military heroes have also played in the game prior to service in war, including William Halsey of Navy, and Omar Bradley and future president Dwight Eisenhower of Army! Ten US presidents have attended the game since Teddy Roosevelt first went in 1901. The traditions in and around the game are special; from the singing of "Almae Matres" to talk of "Beat Army" and "Beat Navy," and so much more, it is a spectacle to behold! There is nothing else quite like Army-Navy because of all that it represents. People from Philly are proud that this grand American game is often played right here! Some year, when you can, try to attend the Army-Navy game!

President John F. Kennedy flips the coin before the 1962 Army-Navy game in Philadelphia. (AP Images)

Connie Mack's Philadelphia A's Win Five World Series

UNTIL THE EAGLES CAPTURED THEIR FIFTH CHAMPIONSHIP in the 2024 NFL season, no Philly professional football, basketball, baseball, or hockey team had won as many titles as the Philadelphia Athletics. The A's, as they were called, were Philly's American League Major League Baseball team in the first half of the 20th century, when the city had two MLB squads, the Phillies and the A's. The A's were often good; the Phils were normally bad, so most Philly sports fans were A's fans back then.

The main figure in A's history was their legendary manager and part-owner, Connie Mack. He began managing the team in 1901, and he did not retire until after the 1950 season, when he was 87 years old! Mack won an incredible 3,731 games (3,582 of them with the A's), which is over 800 more wins than the next closest manager ever! Twice he built powerhouse squads that won back-to-back championships. From 1910 to 1914 the A's featured stars Eddie Collins, Home Run Baker, Eddie Plank, and Charles Bender as they went to four World Series and won two in a row in 1910 and 1911, and then won another title in 1913! Because of money issues, Mack traded away many of his great players after that, so a period of decline set in for the A's.

In the late 1920s, the A's became great again. They reached the World Series in 1929, 1930, and 1931. In '29 and '30 they won it all with some of the very best players to ever play in Philly, such as stars Jimmie Foxx, Al Simmons, Lefty Grove, and Mickey Cochrane. After that, Mack ran into more financial trouble, so again he traded many of his best players. His teams declined in the 1930s, and struggled in the 1940s, and finally after the 1950 season Mack retired due to pressure from those who felt he was too old to be a good manager anymore. In 1954 the A's moved from Philly to Kansas City (later they moved to Oakland; now they play in West Sacramento; in 2028 they may move to Las Vegas). A's fans in Philly were very sad, but in time most became Phillies fans.

Despite a rough end to his career, Mack's legacy of greatness is secure, with nine American League pennants, five World Series titles, the most MLB wins ever, and his election to Baseball's Hall of Fame! Mack remains the only person not associated with the Phillies who is honored with a statue at Citizens Bank Park! The next time you go to a Phils game, look for the statue of "Mr. Mack," which stands along Citizens Bank Way to honor Mack's extraordinary career in Philadelphia!

John B. Kelly, Sr. Brings Glory to Philadelphia in the Olympics

ROWING IS NOT AS POPULAR AS OTHER SPORTS in America, but it has had an impact through the decades in Philadelphia, and this was never truer than when it produced one of Philly's first Olympic champions, John B. Kelly, Sr. Born in 1889, Kelly learned how to row on Philly's Schuylkill River. He honed his skills and developed into a national champion by 1916! But then his rowing career was halted as he served for two years in the US Army in World War I. After the war, Kelly resumed rowing, and got set to test his skills on the world stage at the Henley Royal Regetta, the legendary races along the River Thames in London.

But Kelly was denied entry into Henley, so he pivoted to the 1920 Summer Olympics in Antwerp, Belgium, where he hoped to prove he was the best in the world. In the Olympics, Kelly dazzled. First, in an incredibly close race with only a one-second margin of victory, he won gold in the single sculls by defeating the British champion who had won at Henley! Then, a mere 30 minutes later, Kelly won a second gold in the double sculls! He became the first, and to this day only, athlete to win Olympic gold in both races! And he did it within one hour!

Kelly returned home a hero, with the city celebrating its champion! In 1924 Philly celebrated again when he won another gold in the Summer Olympics in Paris! With his achievements, Kelly helped popularize rowing in Philadelphia, which began hosting the Dad Vail Regatta on the Schuylkill River along Boathouse Row in 1953. Through the years, hundreds of schools and thousands of athletes competed in the Dad Vail in Philly until it moved to New Jersey in 2023.

Kelly, a six-time US champion who won an unbelievable 126 straight races in the single sculls at the height of his career, brought honor to Philadelphia not only though his own achievement, but also with his family's accomplishments through the years. His son, Jack Kelly, Jr., for whom "Kelly Drive" is named, competed in four Olympics and won a bronze medal in 1956! His daughter, Grace Kelly, one of Hollywood's biggest stars, in 1956 became a princess when she married into the Monaco royal family! In 2004, when the Philadelphia Sports Hall of Fame inducted its charter class, Kelly was amongst the 21 individuals honored as he was placed alongside the absolute best of the best in Philly sports history!

Philadelphia Warriors Win Two NBA Championships

BASKETBALL IS A HUGE PART of Philadelphia's sports culture. Years before the 76ers became our pro hoops team in 1963, the Philadelphia Warriors first represented Philly in the NBA. The Warriors competed starting in the 1946–47 season, which the NBA considers its first year of existence. The matter is a bit complicated as the '46–47 Warriors played in a league called the Basketball Association of America. But when the BAA merged with the National Basketball League in 1949, the National

Basketball Association was formed. The NBA decided all records since the 1946–47 BAA season would count as official NBA records.

Eddie Gottlieb ran the Warriors in '46–47 as both coach and GM. The team was good, with a 35–25 regular season record behind strong play from Joe Fulks, who led the squad, averaging 23 points per game. In the playoffs the Warriors got hot. They beat St. Louis and New York to advance to the Finals! The Warriors won three of the first four Finals games, and then in Game 5 on **April 22, 1947,** they defeated the Chicago Stags as Fulks scored 34 points in the clinching game! Because of this, the Philadelphia Warriors are considered the first champion in NBA history!

Three years later in 1950, the Warriors drafted the amazing Paul Arizin out of Villanova. In college, Arizin once scored an incredible 85 points in a game! Arizin was a sensation for the Warriors over his 10-year Hall of Fame career, averaging 22.8 points per game and making the All-Star team each season! He eventually was named to the league's 25th-, 50th-, and 75th-year anniversary squads!

In the 1955–56 season, with Arizin as the star, and with the NBA now a larger part of the American sports landscape, the Warriors went 45–27 in the regular season. Neil Johnston, Joe Graboski, and Tom Gola also contributed in big ways for coach George Senesky's squad. In the playoffs, the Warriors defeated the Syracuse Nationals to get to the Finals! In the NBA Finals against the Fort Wayne Pistons, the Warriors took three of the first four games. Then on **April 7, 1956,** they thrilled Philly sports fans by beating the Pistons 99–88 to win their second NBA title!

Six years later the Warriors saddened their many fans by moving to San Francisco. This opened the way for the formation of the Philadelphia 76ers in 1963.

Wilt Scores 100 Points in a Game

OF ALL THE AMAZING MOMENTS in Philly sports, perhaps nothing is more unbelievable than what Wilt Chamberlain did on March 2, 1962, when he scored 100 points in a game for the Philadelphia Warriors! Playing in Hershey, Pennsylvania, against the Knicks in a game that was not televised, "the Big Dipper" absolutely dominated, while setting the NBA record for most points scored in a game! All these years later, no one has even come close to challenging Wilt's record, and it is likely that no one ever will.

In 1962, Wilt was athletically superior to everyone in basketball. He was taller and stronger than everyone else, and very skilled. On the 100-point night Wilt scored 23 points in the first quarter, and 18 in the second, as Philly led at halftime 79–68. In the third he scored 28 points, for an awesome 69 through three quarters! With one quarter left he needed 31 points to get to 100. The Knicks did not want Wilt to get 100 points, so they began fouling his teammates, hoping other Warriors would score instead of Wilt. As a result, the Warriors started fouling Knicks players in order for New York to shoot free throws so the Warriors would quickly get the ball back. It was a very strange game. Nevertheless, none of New York's tactics could stop Wilt.

With 7:51 to go, Wilt broke his own NBA record with 79 points! With 1:19 left he got to 98! Legendary announcer Bill Campbell called the action for WCAU on the radio: "Rodgers throws long to Chamberlain … he's got it … he is trying to get up … he shoots … no good ... the rebound, Luckenbill … back to Chamberlain … he shoots … up … no good, in and out ... the rebound, Luckenbill … back to Ruklick … in to Chamberlain … he made it! He made it! He made it! A Dipper dunk! He made it! The fans are all over the court! They stop the game! People are running out onto the court! 100 points for Wilt Chamberlain! People are crowding! Warrior players are all over him! Fans are coming out of the stands! The most amazing scoring performance of all time! 100 points for the Big Dipper!"

After the game Wilt held up a "100" sign for what became an iconic photograph. His stats in the win were ridiculous: 48 minutes, 36 of 63 from the field, 28 of 32 from the free throw line, 25 rebounds, two assists, 100 points scored! Wilt set a new standard for greatness, and to

In the most iconic photograph ever taken in Philadelphia sports history, Wilt Chamberlain holds up a "100" sign after scoring a record 100 points in an NBA game. (Paul Vathis/AP Images)

this day is still considered by many people to be the single best player from any sport in Philadelphia sports history!

The Legendary Smokin' Joe Frazier

"HEAVYWEIGHT CHAMPION OF THE WORLD" is perhaps the single greatest title anyone can achieve in sports. Legendary boxer Joe Frazier not only rose through the ranks to claim this title, but he did so fighting out of Philadelphia. "Smokin' Joe," as Frazier was called, had a bruising and relentless style of boxing. He was a brawler. He also was one of Philadelphia's hardest-working and most admired athletes.

Frazier was not born in Philly, but moved to Philadelphia in his early training days. He burst onto the scene winning the heavyweight gold medal in the 1964 Summer Olympics in Tokyo, Japan! In 1965 he turned pro. Frazier won his first fight at Convention Hall in Philly, and then 18 in a row after that! In 1968 he defeated Buster Mathis to become recognized as the champion by the state of New York! Frazier then won four more fights, improving his record to 24–0! This set up a title bout in 1970 against WBA Champion Jimmy Ellis. With Ellis' WBA belt and the WBC belt both on the line, Frazier beat Ellis by way of a technical knockout! Smokin' Joe was the heavyweight champion of the world!

But many people thought Frazier was not actually the best boxer, as former champ Muhammad Ali had previously been stripped of his title for refusing to serve in the Vietnam War. When Ali's boxing license was reinstated, everyone wanted to see the ultimate boxing showdown: the undefeated Muhammad Ali versus the undefeated Joe Frazier! On March 8, 1971, Frazier and Ali fought at Madison Square Garden in New York in what was called "the Fight of the Century." Both fighters battled hard, and in the 15th round Frazier connected with a devastating left hook that sent Ali to the canvas for the first time in his career! Ali got up and continued to fight, but when it was all over Frazier won the decision on all three judge's scorecards! Smokin' Joe had won the Fight of the Century!

Frazier continued to fight for 10 more years, winning some incredible bouts and twice losing in a loaded heavyweight division to both George Foreman and to Ali when they fought again. He retired in 1981. To this day, Frazier remains the only fighter out of Philadelphia to win an Olympic gold medal and the heavyweight title! Smokin' Joe is one of boxing—and one of Philly's—all-time greats!

Joe Frazier knocks down Muhammad Ali in the 15th round of "the Fight of the Century." (David Hume Kennerly/Bettmann via Getty Images)

Cathy Rush Leads Immaculata to a Three-Peat

DECADES BEFORE WOMEN'S COLLEGE HOOPS rose in stature to the level it is at today, Immaculata College, a suburban-Philadelphia school, accomplished the awesome feat of winning the first three national championships in women's college basketball history! Their story, one of skill and incredible grit, inspired girls, boys, and adults with their championship achievement as they advanced women's sports.

Immaculata had tough obstacles to overcome: they had less than 600 students; their gym burned down; they had no scholarships; players wore one set of wool tunics as uniforms, which they washed in a hotel sink on the road; and there was no budget to send them to a postseason tournament. But they had Cathy Rush, a tremendous coach, and terrific players such as Theresa Shank. And in the 1971–72 season they had a shot at national glory because for the first time there would be a postseason tournament for women's college basketball. That season, "the Macs," as they were known, excelled, going 20–1 prior to the AIAW Tournament. The tournament, in Normal, Illinois, was attended by only five Immaculata student fans. Nevertheless, Rush's team won three straight games to advance to the title game! On **March 19, 1972,** the Macs defeated West Chester 52–48 to win the national championship! When they got home thousands of fans greeted them! The Macs became a sensation. Given the moniker "Mighty Macs," Rush's squad was hungry for more. The next year they added standout Marianne Crawford, and went back to the title game. On **March 24, 1973,** they made it back-to-back championships, defeating Queens College 59–52! Remarkably, the following year the Mighty Macs did it again, beating Mississippi 68–53 on **March 23, 1974,** for a three-peat!

With their success, Immaculata became the first US women's team to play overseas, and they played in the first national TV game featuring women players! Rush retired after the '77 season with six Final Four appearances, three titles, and an awesome 149–15 record! She has taught hoops for years at her camps, helping thousands of youngsters become better players. Rush was inducted into the Basketball Hall of Fame in 2008! And in 2014 the entire Mighty Macs squad was inducted into the Hall! Immaculata's story was even turned into a film! When you get a chance, watch *The Mighty Macs*, a movie about these amazing women!

The Remarkable Carl Lewis

WITH THIS STORY WE ARE GOING TO STRETCH THE BOUNDS of "Philadelphia sports" a bit, focusing on the remarkable Carl Lewis, who grew up in Willingboro, New Jersey, just outside of Philly. Lewis, a member of the Philadelphia Sports Hall of Fame, was so dominant in track and field with his blazing speed and awe-inspiring leaping ability that no 20th century athlete won more Olympic gold medals than he did!

Lewis starred at Willingboro High School, where he was particularly great in the long jump. He then excelled for the University of Houston as an All-American and NCAA champion! But it was on the international stage that Lewis made his biggest mark, and this was never truer than in the 1984 Summer Olympics in Los Angeles. Representing the US in his home country, Lewis was the star of stars, as he set out to equal the great Jesse Owens' sensational feat of capturing four gold medals in the 1936 Summer Olympics. In '84, Lewis won his first gold in the 100-meter race! He followed that up by claiming gold in the long jump! Then he won the 200 meter! Finally, Lewis anchored the Men's 4x100 meter relay race, setting a new world record, as he amazed and thrilled the nation by winning his fourth gold medal!

Lewis, so talented in 1984, was even selected that year by the Cowboys in the NFL Draft and by the Bulls in the NBA Draft (same draft as Michael Jordan)!

Carl Lewis was at the height of his career during the 1984 Summer Olympics in Los Angeles. (David Madison/Getty Images)

Lewis' Olympic success was far from over. In 1988 he won gold in the 100-meter and the long jump! In 1992 he won gold in the long jump and the 4x100! Then in 1996, incredibly at the age of 35, Lewis made history by winning the long jump in his fourth straight Olympiad, while tying swimmer Mark Spitz's record for the most gold medals with nine! Fans in New Jersey, Philadelphia, and beyond cheered Lewis' achievement!

Lewis also won eight world championships and set numerous world records, including two of them in the 100-meter! His personal best of 9.86 seconds at the age of 30 was stunning! He once jumped 29 feet 2¾ inches in the long jump (try it to see how far you can get)! For 10 years he was unbeaten in the long jump! He was named "Olympian of the Century" by *Sports Illustrated*, and "Sportsman of the Century" by the International Olympic Committee! For all of this and more, Lewis is considered one of the very best athletes from any sport of all time!

Smarty Jones' Magical Run in the Kentucky Derby and Preakness

IN 2004, SPORTS FANS TURNED THEIR ATTENTION to an underdog Philadelphia horse named Smarty Jones, who had risen the ranks to appear on horse racing's greatest stage, the Kentucky Derby. What Smarty did next made him a legend.

To this day, fans who saw Smarty race still remember his improbable, magical and inspirational journey as this small racehorse overcame such long odds to become a true Philadelphia champion. The year before rising to stardom though, Smarty suffered a devastating injury when he smashed his head into a gate. Smarty fell to the ground unconscious, bleeding heavily from his head with a life-threatening fractured skull. Fortunately, Smarty was given great care, and in time he overcame his injuries to regain his health and strength. Owned by Roy and Pat Chapman, Smarty, trained by John Servis, was able to start racing competitively out of Philadelphia Park. Smarty won his first race. Then he won his second and third. Smarty followed that up with three more wins, raising his record to 6–0! The Chapmans and Servis entered Smarty into horse racing's greatest event, the Kentucky Derby.

May 1, 2004, was a proud day for fans as a Philadelphia horse was in the Derby, but what happened in the race was even better. Smarty fell behind early, but with jockey Stewart Elliott guiding him, Smarty caught up to the lead horse, Lion Heart, along the backstretch. Smarty and Lion Heart sprinted neck and neck, and with rain coming down hard Smarty pulled away, finishing first to win the Kentucky Derby! He became the first undefeated Derby winner since Seattle Slew in 1977!

Smarty had become a star, and he appeared on the cover of *Sports Illustrated*! Now fans wanted to see him in the Preakness Stakes, the second leg of horse racing's Triple Crown. In the Preakness, after dropping behind, Elliott raced Smarty to the front, and as Smarty continued to surge he pulled away to win by a huge margin! Smarty was just one win away from the Triple Crown! Unfortunately, in the Belmont Stakes, Smarty was tired from running three races in just five weeks, and he lost at the very end to Birdstone. It was a disappointing end, but everyone knew Smarty had already given us so many thrills. He proved to be one of the best horses ever, and an inspiration who captured the hearts of Philly sports fans!

Jockey Stewart Elliott rides Smarty Jones to victory in the 2004 Kentucky Derby. (Al Behrman/AP Images)

The Amazing Bernard Hopkins

IT IS POSSIBLE THAT NO PHILADELPHIA ATHLETE has had a more complicated road to glory or demonstrated a more determined spirit overcoming odds than the amazing Bernard Hopkins. Hopkins' story is one of tragedy, big mistakes, and tremendous triumph. He saw crime as a kid growing up in Philly, and engaged in criminal activity himself as a teenager. At the age of 17 he was sentenced to 18 years in prison. While in prison, Hopkins decided to turn his life around. He also discovered a love of boxing. After five years behind bars, Hopkins was released from prison in 1988. He set out for a career in boxing.

"B-Hop" lost his first pro fight, but he improved as he learned the fight game, winning 22 bouts in a row! In 1993 he lost a championship match to Roy Jones, Jr., but over the next two years set up another title bout. In 1995 Hopkins won the IBF middleweight title! With a style based on defense, counter-punching skills, savvy, and power, "the Executioner" made a record 20 title defenses as a middleweight! In 2001 he unified the middleweight division and became the lineal champion, defeating the great Felix Trinidad with an upset victory! In 2004 he beat Oscar De La Hoya to become the undisputed champion! B-Hop was the first middleweight to hold titles in all four major sanctioning bodies at the same time!

Hopkins' success as a middleweight was remarkable, as he lost only one fight from 1990 through February 2005! His middleweight run finally ended with two losses to Jermain Taylor. People thought Hopkins' days of greatness were over, but with superb mental and physical discipline, he stayed in shape and decided to become a light heavyweight. Incredibly, in his next bout Hopkins won the light heavyweight title, defeating Antonio Tarver! Five years later, at the age of 46, he set a record, becoming the oldest fighter to win a belt! After that, with each victory B-Hop set a new age record as champ! He was even champion at the age of 49! Hopkins finally retired in his early 50s after a sensational 29-year career! His accomplishments had been extraordinary: WBC, WBA, WBO, IBF, and lineal middleweight champion; WBC, WBA, IBF, and lineal light heavyweight champion! His journey from a troubled childhood to a life and career of redemption was an inspiration. Hopkins is one of boxing's best ever, and one of Philly's most dominant athletes in any sport!

Mo'ne Davis Stars in the Little League World Series

PHILADELPHIA HAS HAD SOME AMAZING SPORTS STORIES, and one of the most unique and inspiring was when a 13-year old girl named Mo'ne Davis starred for the Taney Dragons in the Little League World Series! This was the story of a girl proving she could play with the boys, and the boys and that girl proving they were one of the top Little League teams in the nation.

Until 2014, the Dragons had never been to the Little League World Series. It is very hard to get there, as each year thousands of American teams compete, trying to get one of only eight United States spots in the tournament, which is held in Williamsport, Pennsylvania. But the 2014 Dragons, featuring 12 players from Philly, were a fantastic team that season. In August, needing only one more win to make it to Williamsport, Mo'ne pitched a three-hit shutout, helping the Dragons secure the Mid-Atlantic title! The kids were headed to the Little League World Series!

When Philly sports fans and people all over the nation realized the team's best player was Mo'ne, a girl, millions started rooting for her and the Dragons. In Williamsport, playing live on ESPN, Mo'ne did not disappoint. Becoming only the fourth US girl to play in the Little League World Series, she dominated against Nashville, striking out eight batters while pitching a two-hit shutout! This was the first shoutout ever by a girl in the Little League World Series! In their next game, Mo'ne got a base hit in another Dragons win! Each game was attracting a huge audience on TV. Some of Mo'ne's games set a record for the most-watched Little League World Series game ever up to that point! Mo'ne was a star!

Sadly, the Dragons were eliminated in the semifinals of the US bracket. But praise for Mo'ne poured in. She was featured on the cover of *Sports Illustrated* with a photo of her pitching and "Mo'ne" written in big letters, and a sub-headline that said: "Remember Her Name (As

Mo'ne Davis inspired millions of people with her performance in the 2014 Little League World Series. (Gene J. Puskar/AP Images)

If We Could Ever Forget)!" Her jersey was sent to the Baseball Hall of Fame! Many famous people, including then–first lady Michelle Obama, tweeted congratulations to her! And Mo'ne won the ESPY Award for Best Breakthrough Athlete! By proving she could play and excel with and against boys, while handling all the pressure and attention in Williamsport with tremendous grace and humility, Mo'ne entertained and inspired millions of people! Philadelphia sports fans were extremely proud that Mo'ne was one of our own!

Carli Lloyd Dominates on the World Stage

WITH THIS STORY WE ARE GOING TO AGAIN EXTEND the reach of Philadelphia sports a tad, focusing on the remarkable Carli Lloyd, one of America's greatest soccer players, who grew up just outside of Philly in New Jersey. After starring at Delran High School and Rutgers University, Lloyd played for various teams for close to two decades in Women's Professional Soccer (WPS), the National Women's Soccer League (NWSL), and the FA Women's Super League in England. But it is what she did on the international stage representing the United States that made her a legend.

After playing for the U-21 American team, Lloyd made her debut with the US National Soccer Team in 2005 at the age of 22. Three years later she was the US Soccer Player of the Year and won a gold medal with Team USA in the 2008 Summer Olympics in Beijing! She scored the winning goal in extra time in the gold medal game! Unbelievably, four years later she again scored the winning goal in the gold medal game in the 2012 Summer Olympics in London! Lloyd is the only player ever to score the winning goal in two different Olympic finals! She had become a major star!

Her World Cup success was also amazing. In 2007 she played in her first World Cup, with the US finishing in third place. In 2011 the US finished in second place. In the 2015 World Cup final against Japan, with Lloyd playing perhaps the best soccer of her career, she scored a stunning three goals in the first 16 minutes of the game! Americans were thrilled to see one player dominate so much! After the 5–2 US win, Lloyd won the Golden Ball Trophy as the World Cup's best player! When Lloyd and her teammates returned to America they were given a ticker-tape parade in New York City, becoming the first women's soccer team to receive such an honor! Incredibly, four years later, Lloyd helped the US win another World Cup!

One of the most clutch players ever, Lloyd is a source of pride for people from New Jersey, Philly, and beyond. Her career was phenomenal: four Olympics, two Olympic golds, a US record 10 Olympic goals, four World Cups, two World Cup titles, two-time FIFA Player of the Year, and the third most goals and fifth most assists ever for the US National Soccer Team! Lloyd, who growing up was a huge Philly sports fan, as an adult became one of the greatest athletes ever from our area!

The Champion Spirit of Dawn Staley

OUR FINAL CHAPTER FOCUSES ON THE REMARKABLE DAWN STALEY, one of the most accomplished basketball players and coaches to ever come from Philadelphia. Some of her success occurred outside of Philly, but Staley, from North Philadelphia, has always carried the determined spirit of Philly with her every step of the way.

She starred at Dobbins Tech, and was named the National High School Player of the Year her senior year in 1988! In college Staley excelled for the University of Virginia with averages of 16.3 points, 5.9 rebounds, 5.6 assists, and 3.5 steals per game. Her 454 steals set an NCAA record! She also led Virginia to three Final Four appearances and was named the 1991 Final Four Most Outstanding Player! Twice she won the Naismith Award as the National Player of the Year!

Dawn Staley celebrates one of her four Olympic gold medals representing Team USA. (Elise Amendola/AP Images)

When Staley graduated in 1992, the WNBA did not exist yet, so she began her pro career playing overseas. After that, Staley played in the American Basketball League for two years, and then was drafted in the 1999 WNBA Draft. With her aggressive, smart, and tough playing style, Staley became a five-time WNBA All-Star! Incredibly, while still playing in the WNBA, she became the head coach of Temple in 2000! Yes, part of the year she would play, and part of the year she would coach! In her eight seasons back in Philly with the Owls, Staley led Temple to a 172–80 record and six NCAA Tournaments! In 2008 she became the head coach of South Carolina, where Staley achieved even more success. Four times named the Naismith National Coach of the Year, Staley has reached the Final Four seven times with South Carolina, and won an amazing three national championships! Her 2024 squad even went undefeated! Plus, Staley is the only person ever to win a Naismith award as a player and a coach!

Staley has also starred representing the United States on the world stage. As a player she won a gold medal in the 1996, 2000, and 2004 Summer Olympics! In '04 Staley even carried the US flag during the Opening Ceremony! As a head coach she won gold in the 2021 Summer Olympics in Tokyo! Staley, who feels pride being from Philly, was inducted into the Basketball Hall of Fame in 2013! She is one of our all-time greats, and there are some, like the author of this book, who hope someday she becomes the head coach of the 76ers.

ADDENDUM

Philadelphia Sports Hall of Famers

IN 2002, *PHILADELPHIA INQUIRER* COLUMNIST Frank Fitzpatrick wrote an article advocating that Philadelphia should have a sports hall of fame. The day the story was published, Philly sports fan Ken Avalon read the article and quickly got moving to turn the hall of fame concept into reality. The formation of the Philadelphia Sports Hall of Fame was announced to the public in 2003. The charter class of hall of famers was inducted in 2004. Each year the Hall honors high-achieving individuals and teams worthy of recognition with a gala event. It is a wonderful part of our Philadelphia sports community, and will serve as a lasting legacy for those enshrined.

The Hall recognizes not only those who played, coached, or were an executive/owner for one of the Philly teams, but also honors individuals who grew up in our area and then excelled elsewhere. The Hall also honors officials, broadcasters, writers, venues, and special contributors.

Here are the members of the Philadelphia Sports Hall of Fame:

Charter Class: 2004	
Richie Ashburn	Baseball
Steve Carlton	Baseball
Jimmie Foxx	Baseball
Connie Mack	Baseball
Robin Roberts	Baseball
Mike Schmidt	Baseball
Paul Arizin	Basketball
Wilt Chamberlain	Basketball
Billy Cunningham	Basketball
Julius Erving	Basketball
Tom Gola	Basketball
Joe Frazier	Boxing
Chuck Bednarik	Football
Bert Bell	Football
Steve Van Buren	Football
Bernie Parent	Hockey
Bobby Clarke	Hockey
John B. Kelly, Sr.	Rowing
Bill Tilden	Tennis
Harry Kalas	Legacy of Excellence
Sonny Hill	Lifetime Commitment

2nd Class: 2005	
Grover Cleveland Alexander	Baseball
Lefty Grove	Baseball
1954 La Salle Explorers	Basketball
Charles Barkley	Basketball
John Chaney	Basketball
Eddie Gottlieb	Basketball
Guy Rodgers	Basketball
Cathy Rush	Basketball
Tommy McDonald	Football
Pete Pihos	Football
Robert Jay Sigel	Golf
James "Jumbo" Elliott	Track and Field
Carl Lewis	Track and Field
Joe Verdeur	Swimming / Diving
Vic Seixas	Tennis
Bill Campbell	Legacy of Excellence
Harvey Pollack	Legacy of Excellence
Bob Levy	Lifetime Commitment
Ed Snider	Philadelphia Medal

3rd Class: 2006	
Roy Campanella	Baseball
Del Ennis	Baseball
Reggie Jackson	Baseball
Al Simmons	Baseball
Joe Fulks	Basketball
Hal Greer	Basketball
Dr. Jack Ramsay	Basketball
William Joseph Mosconi	Billiards
Anne Townsend	Field Hockey
1960 Philadelphia Eagles	Football
Herb Adderley	Football
Helen Sigel Wilson	Golf
Don Bragg	Track and Field
Ray Didinger	Legacy of Excellence
Gene Hart	Legacy of Excellence
Bill Ellerbee	Lifetime Commitment
The Palestra	Venue Enshrinement

4th Class: 2007	
1980 Philadelphia Phillies	Baseball
Mickey Cochrane	Baseball
Chuck Klein	Baseball
Theresa Shank Grentz	Basketball
Harry Litwack	Basketball
Earl Monroe	Basketball
Beth Anders	Field Hockey
Frank "Bucko" Kilroy	Football
Earle "Greasy" Neale	Football
Reggie White	Football
Bill Barber	Hockey
Walter Bahr	Soccer
Bill Lyon	Legacy of Excellence
Jack Whitaker	Legacy of Excellence

5th Class: 2008	
1929–30 Philadelphia As	Baseball
Ed Delahanty	Baseball
Mickey Vernon	Baseball
Maurice Cheeks	Basketball
Herb Magee	Basketball
Lionel Simmons	Basketball
Tommy Loughran	Boxing
Harold Carmichael	Football
Al Wistert	Football
Dorothy Porter	Golf
Fred Shero	Hockey
Leroy Burrell	Track and Field
Stan Hochman	Legacy of Excellence

6th Class: 2009	
Larry Bowa	Baseball
Eddie Collins	Baseball
Julius "Judy" Johnson	Baseball
Tommy Lasorda	Baseball
Neil Johnston	Basketball
Joey Giardello	Boxing
Betty Shellenberger	Field Hockey
John Cappelletti	Football
Pete Retzlaff	Football
Emlen Tunnell	Football
1973–74 and 1974–75 Flyers	Hockey
Dr. Charles Jenkins	Track and Field
Mel Sheppard	Track and Field
Bill Conlin	Legacy of Excellence
Merrill Reese	Legacy of Excellence

7th Class: 2010	
Dick Allen	Baseball
Tug McGraw	Baseball
Bobby Shantz	Baseball
Bobby Jones	Basketball
Jim Phelan	Basketball
Marianne Crawford Stanley	Basketball
"Jersey" Joe Walcott	Boxing
Tom Brookshier	Football
Leroy Kelly	Football
Mike Quick	Football
William Hyndman III	Golf
Hobey Baker	Hockey
Ron Hextall	Hockey
Elizabeth Becker	Swimming / Diving
Phil Jasner	Legacy of Excellence
Lighthouse Boys Soccer Club	Lifetime Commitment

8th Class: 2011	
Jimmy Dykes	Baseball
Biz Mackey	Baseball
Joe McCarthy	Baseball
Curt Simmons	Baseball
Moses Malone	Basketball
Dawn Staley	Basketball
Bill Bergey	Football
Wilbert Montgomery	Football
Mark Howe	Hockey
Ora Washington	Tennis
Ted Meredith	Track and Field
Al Meltzer	Legacy of Excellence
Speedy Morris	Lifetime Commitment
Ed Sabol	Philadelphia Medal
Steve Sabol	Philadelphia Medal
Penn Relays	Special Enshrinement

9th Class: 2012	
Johnny Callison	Baseball
Gertrude Dunn	Baseball
Mike Piazza	Baseball
Eddie Plank	Baseball
Doug Collins	Basketball
Debbie Black	Basketball
Wali Jones	Basketball
Harold Johnson	Boxing
Maxie Baughan	Football
Joe Klecko	Football
Tommy Thompson	Football
Johnny McDermott	Golf
Eric Lindros	Hockey
Horace Ashenfelter	Track and Field
Dan Baker	Legacy of Excellence
Legacy Youth Tennis and Education	Lifetime Commitment

10th Class: 2013	
Shag Crawford	Baseball
Greg Luzinski	Baseball
Bucky Walters	Baseball
Geno Auriemma	Basketball
Michael Brooks	Basketball
Ernie Beck	Basketball
Linda Page	Basketball
Andrew Toney	Basketball
Bob Brown	Football
Eddie George	Football
Dave Robinson	Football
John LeClair	Hockey
Tina Sloan Green	Lacrosse
Joe Burk	Rowing
Carl Robie	Swimming / Diving
Joe Hand, Sr.	Legacy of Excellence
Pat Williams	Legacy of Excellence

11th Class: 2014	
Charles "Chief" Bender	Baseball
Herb Pennock	Baseball
Curt Schilling	Baseball
Immaculata "Mighty Macs"	Basketball
Geoff Petrie	Basketball
Chet Walker	Basketball
Meldrick Taylor	Boxing
Eric Allen	Football
Marvin Harrison	Football
Bobby Walston	Football
Brian Propp	Hockey
Mike Richter	Hockey
Paul Costello	Rowing
Ellie Daniel	Swimming / Diving
Jean Shiley	Track and Field
Frank Dolson	Legacy of Excellence
Byrum "By" Saam	Legacy of Excellence

12th Class: 2015	
Garry Maddox	Baseball
Sam Thompson	Baseball
Walt Hazzard	Basketball
Bob Montgomery	Boxing
Karen Shelton	Field Hockey
Timmy Brown	Football
Rich Gannon	Football
Dick Vermeil	Football
Rick MacLeish	Hockey
Lou Nolan	Hockey
Cindy Timchal	Lacrosse
Benny McLaughin	Soccer
R. Norris "Dick" Williams	Tennis
Dave Zinkoff	Legacy of Excellence
Billy Markward	Lifetime Commitment

13th Class: 2016	
Goose Goslin	Baseball
Charlie Manuel	Baseball
Chris Short	Baseball
1966–67 Philadelphia 76ers	Basketball
Al Severance	Basketball
Marilyn Stephens	Basketball
Jeff Chandler	Boxing
Sylvia Wene Martin	Boxing
Vonnie Gros	Field Hockey
Brian Dawkins	Football
Jimmy Watson	Hockey
Bruce Harlan	Swimming / Diving
George Orton	Track and Field
Steve Fredericks	Legacy of Excellence
Herman Taylor	Legacy of Excellence
Dick "Hoops" Weiss	Legacy of Excellence

14th Class: 2017	
Bob Boone	Baseball
Granny Hamner	Baseball
Bob Johnson	Baseball
Mike Bantom	Basketball
Rene Portland	Basketball
Ray Scott	Basketball
"Philadelphia" Jack O'Brien	Boxing
Randall Cunningham	Football
Ron Jaworski	Football
Tim Kerr	Hockey
John B. "Jack" Kelly	Rowing
Irene Guest	Swimming / Diving
Donald Hunt	Legacy of Excellence
Andrea Kremer	Legacy of Excellence
The Army-Navy Game	Special Enshrinement

15th Class: 2018	
Gavvy Cravath	Baseball
Danny Murtaugh	Baseball
Jamie Moyer	Baseball
Louis Santop	Baseball
Allen Iverson	Basketball
Muffett McGraw	Basketball
Benny Bass	Boxing
1948 and 1949 Eagles	Football
Billy "White Shoes" Johnson	Football
Brian Westbrook	Football
Reggie Leach	Hockey
Joanne Iverson	Rowing
David Berkoff	Swimming / Diving
Donald Lippincott	Track and Field
Mel Greenberg	Legacy of Excellence
Claire Smith	Legacy of Excellence

16th Class: 2019	
Frank "Home Run" Baker	Baseball
Paul Owens	Baseball
Mike Scioscia	Baseball
Fran Dunphy	Basketball
Bill Melchionni	Basketball
Rasheed Wallace	Basketball
Matthew Saad Muhammad	Boxing
Charlene Morett	Field Hockey
Donovan McNabb	Football
Troy Vincent	Football
Clara Schroth-Lomady	Gymnastics
Éric Desjardins	Hockey
Al Cantello	Track and Field
Suzy Kolber	Legacy of Excellence
Jayson Stark	Legacy of Excellence

17th Class: 2020	
1910 –13 Philadelphia As	Baseball
Cy Williams	Baseball
Kobe Bryant	Basketball
Bo Ryan	Basketball
Earl Strom	Basketball
Tim Witherspoon	Boxing
Deron Cherry	Football
Vic Sears	Football
Jerry Sisemore	Football
Rick Tocchet	Hockey
Cherie Greer Brown	Lacrosse
Bob Rigby	Soccer
Lisa Raymond	Tennis
Herman Frazier	Track and Field
David Montgomery	Legacy of Excellence
J. Russell Peltz	Legacy of Excellence
Ken Hamilton	Lifetime Commitment

18th Class: 2021	
Dallas Green	Baseball
1947 Philadelphia Warriors	Basketball
"Zack" Clayton	Basketball
Larry Foust	Basketball
Richard Hamilton	Basketball
Yolanda Laney	Basketball
Lew Tendler	Boxing
Bill Bradley	Football
Seth Joyner	Football
Jim Katcavage	Football
"Kid" Keinath	Football
Mark Recchi	Hockey
Bonnie Rosen	Lacrosse
Mike Teti	Rowing
Olga Dorfner	Swimming / Diving
Gary Smith	Legacy of Excellence

19th Class: 2022	
Ed Bolden	Baseball
Jimmy Rollins	Baseball
1982–83 76ers	Basketball
Charles Cooper	Basketball
Phil Martelli	Basketball
Rollie Massimino	Basketball
Nikki Franke	Fencing
Adele Boyd	Field Hockey
David Akers	Football
Francis "Reds" Bagnell	Football
Art McNally	Football
Keith Allen	Hockey
Fredia Gibbs	Mixed Martial Arts
Susan Francia	Rowing
Howard Eskin	Legacy of Excellence
Ray Kelly	Legacy of Excellence
The Blue Horizon	Venue Enshrinement

20th Class: 2023	
Willie Jones	Baseball
Carlos Ruiz	Baseball
Valerie Still	Basketball
Jay Wright	Basketball
Bernard Hopkins	Boxing
Irving Fryar	Football
Truxton Hare	Football
Jeremiah Trotter	Football
Anthony Black	Horse Racing
Joe Watson	Hockey
Al Holbert	Motor Sports
Bill Knecht	Rowing
Judy Auritt Klein	Swimming / Diving
Carol Lewis	Track and Field
Bill Giles	Legacy of Excellence
James Isaminger	Legacy of Excellence

21st Class: 2024	
Ryan Howard	Baseball
Eddie Stanky	Baseball
Chase Utley	Baseball
Jameer Nelson	Basketball
Cheryl Reeve	Basketball
Paul Westhead	Basketball
George Benton	Boxing
Alice Putnam Willetts	Field Hockey
Andy Talley	Football
Stan Walters	Football
A.W. Tillinghast	Golf
Joan Moore Gnat	Gymnastics
Rod Brind'Amour	Hockey
Brendan Hansen	Swimming
Angelo Cataldi	Legacy of Excellence
Lurline Jones	Lifetime Commitment

22nd Class: 2025	
1925 Darby Hilldales	Baseball
Roy Thomas	Baseball
1985 Villanova Wildcats	Basketball
Mendy Rudolph	Basketball
Gary Williams	Basketball
Dwight Muhammad Qawi	Boxing
Mike Rozier	Football
Clyde Simmons	Football
Paul Holmgren	Hockey
Virginia Allen	Lacrosse
Christy Morgan	Lacrosse
Eddie Coyle	Paralympic Powerlifting
Mary Ellen Clark	Swimming / Diving
Bo Roberson	Track & Field + Football
Lynne Carter	Legacy of Excellence
Dick Jerardi	Legacy of Excellence
Allen Lewis	Legacy of Excellence
Jeffrey Lurie	Philadelphia Medal

Are you going to be a future Philadelphia Sports Hall of Famer? Maybe. Regardless, enjoy being a fan. There is so much to love about Philly sports!

Thank you so much for reading this book. I hope you enjoyed it!

—Joe DeCamara